Helen Van Wyk's Favorite
Color Recipes 2

Books by Helen Van Wyk

Casselwyk Book On Oil Painting
Basic Oil Painting The Van Wyk Way
  (Revision of *Casselwyk Book On Oil Painting*)

Acrylic Portrait Painting (out of print)
Successful Color Mixtures
Helen Van Wyk's Favorite Color Recipes
Helen Van Wyk's Favorite Color Recipes 2
  (Revisions of *Successful Color Mixtures*)

Painting Flowers The Van Wyk Way
Portraits In Oil The Van Wyk Way
Your Painting Questions Answered From A To Z
Welcome To My Studio
Welcome To My Studio (New Revised Edition)

Color Mixing in Action
My 13 Colors And How I Use Them
Color Mixing The Van Wyk Way
  (Combines *Color Mixing in Action* and *My 13 Colors*)

HELEN VAN WYK'S FAVORITE COLOR RECIPES 2
by Helen Van Wyk
Paperback edition copyright © 2001
by Art Instruction Associates
Sarasota, Florida 34233 USA

Parts of this book were published earlier as
Successful Color Mixtures, by Helen Van Wyk

Published by Art Instruction Associates
5361 Kelly Drive, Sarasota, Florida 34233 USA

ISBN 0-929552-21-0

06 05 04 03 02   6 5 4 3 2

Distributed to the book trade and art trade in the U.S. by
North Light Books, an imprint of F&W Publications
4700 East Galbraith Road, Cincinnati, Ohio 45236 USA
Telephone: 513-531-2690, 800-289-0963

Additional Illustrations and Text by Laura Elkins Stover

Edited by Herb Rogoff

Art Direction by Stephen Bridges

Design by Stephen Bridges and Laura Herrmann

Indexing by Ann Fleury

Project coordinated by Hand Books Press
2 Briarstone Road, Rockport, MA 01966 USA

Printed in China

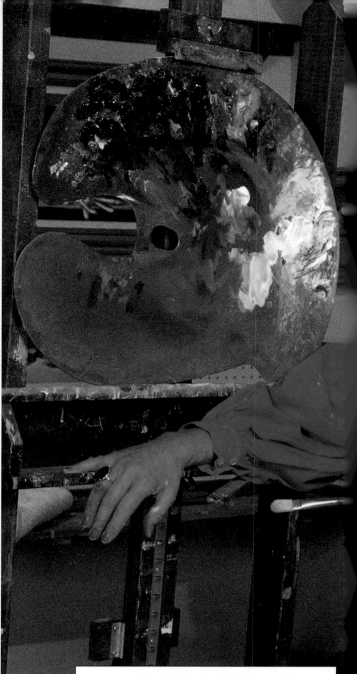

Metric Conversion Chart

To Convert	To	Multiply By
Inches	Centimeters	2.54
Centimeters	Inches	0.4
Feet	Centimeters	30.5
Centimeters	Feet	0.03
Yards	Meters	0.9
Meters	Yards	1.1
Sq. Inches	Sq. Centimeters	6.45
Sq. Centimeters	Sq. Inches	0.16
Sq. Feet	Sq. Meters	0.09
Sq. Meters	Sq. Feet	10.8
Sq. Yards	Sq. Meters	0.08
Sq. Meters	Sq. Yards	1.2
Pounds	Kilograms	0.45
Kilograms	Pounds	2.2
Ounces	Grams	28.4
Grams	Ounces	0.04

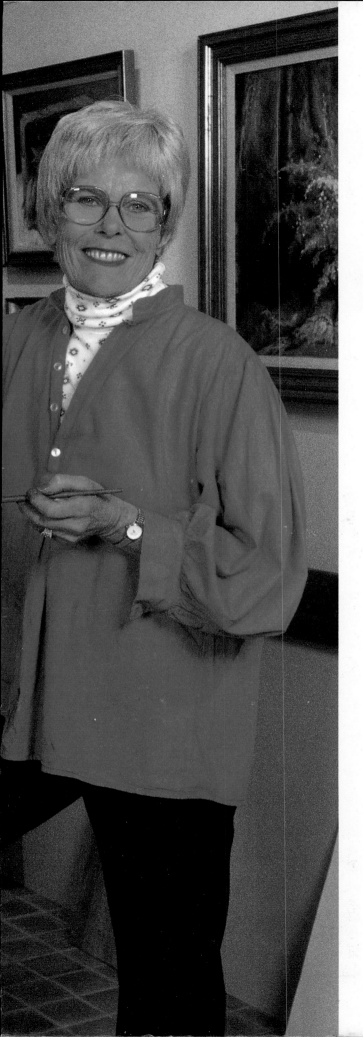

Helen Van Wyk's Favorite
Color Recipes 2

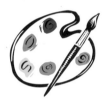

By Helen Van Wyk

Art Instruction Associates
Sarasota, Florida

Distributed by North Light Books
Cincinnati, Ohio

Table of Contents

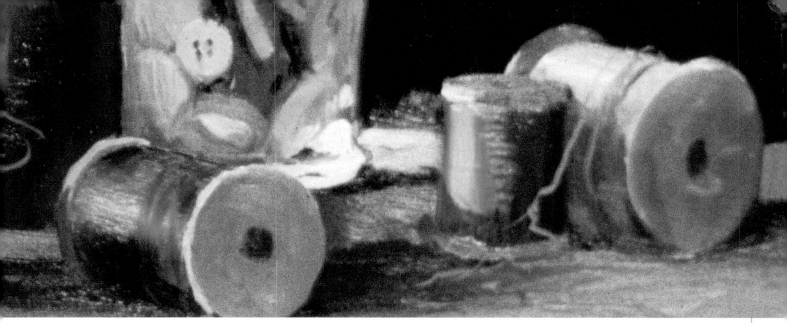

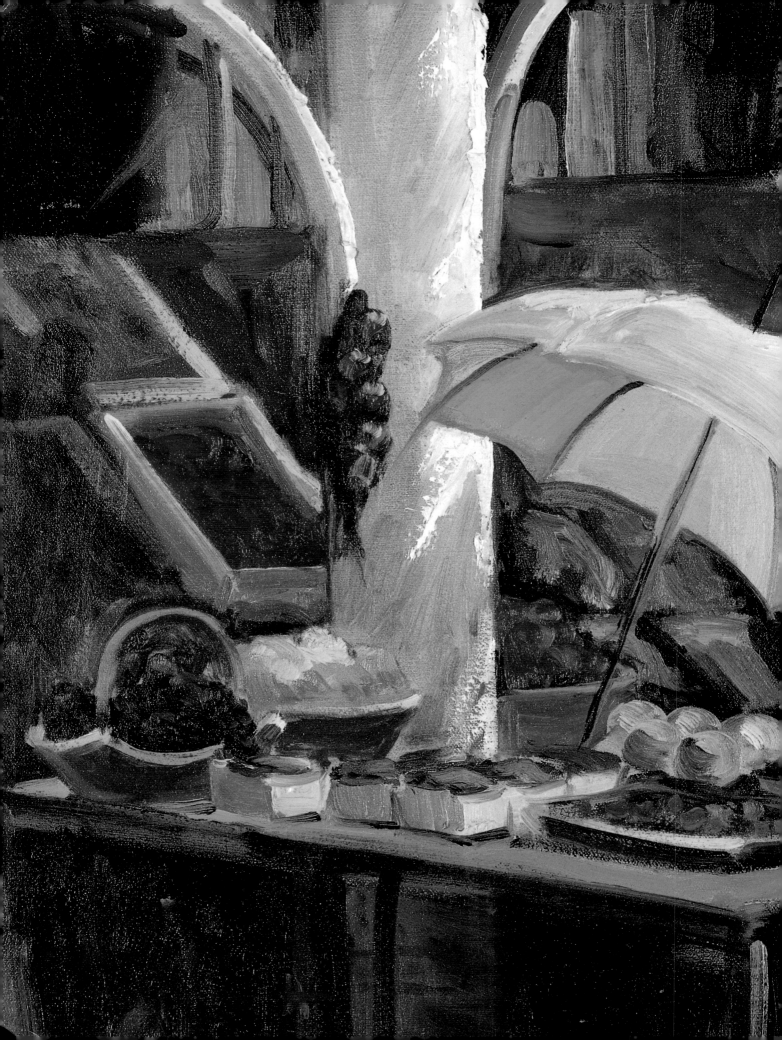

Introduction

Liberally sprinkled throughout Helen Van Wyk's books, lectures and demonstrations are pearls of wisdom which, in the extraordinary astuteness which she possessed, she mostly credited to her teacher and mentor, M. A. Rasko. And those words, which she readily admitted Rasko *never* said, she credited to her mother, Alida DeBoer. In truth, those two individuals, significant in Helen's life, did not make *all* the statements for which she publicly gave them credit. Helen unselfishly attributed to them many profound observations in the belief that out of their minds, older and revered, their words would carry more credence with her students, audiences and readers. I will not here, nor anywhere else, ever reveal which quotes were truly Rasko/Mom and which were the brilliant perceptions of Helen herself.

One comment that Rasko *did* make was his reaction to Helen's first published book back in 1961, when she presented him with a copy. Flipping through the 120 pages of the book, *The Casselwyk Book on Oil Painting,* Rasko said, "The study of the three-dimensional expression on the two-dimensional surface consists of sixteen pages, no more no less." His pronouncement was indeed dogmatic, but one, I suspect, that was said with tongue in cheek. I assume that upon seeing Helen's first published effort, her mentor, gravely ill at that time, became concerned that his most treasured student would lose her sense of humility. Anyone who was ever associated with Helen Van Wyk would know that Rasko had nothing to fear. I am certain that he did, too. Helen always knew that Rasko was proud of her; she knew at this time that he was proud of her book.

Sixteen pages? That's not far-fetched since the principles of painting could logically consume that amount of space in print, give or take a few pages. But when you consider how vast the study of this craft truly is, and how much each author-painter has to say to those many aspirants with brush in hand, canvas in place, I can tell you that there's always room for more books by Helen Van Wyk; they are always received so tumultuously by her fans.

All that you have just read, in this introduction, is my way of letting you know why we — Art Instruction Associates — felt the need to publish this sequel to the highly successful, highly acclaimed and still-very-much-in-circulation *Helen Van Wyk's Favorite Color Recipes*.

Not only have we added more *Recipes*, written in the same cookbook style as the first book, but we have included additional sections that formed the framework of Helen's painting and teaching philosophy. They are essential to the study of painting.

One of them (Section III) is all about composition and in it, through a number of examples, Helen demonstrates why the success of any painting starts with the first lines that design the composition.

In another section (IV), Helen discusses painting procedures: how to start, how to proceed and how to finish. She stresses working from the top down, starting in the area farthest back and moving forward; how brushstrokes, blending edges of shadows, and many other devices can make your paintings look plausible.

Section V is one that all people who paint realistically want to learn and master. It's all about textures, what they are and how to get them to look real.

We are proud of this book. We are confident that Mr. Rasko would be too and, what is more important, so would Helen.

Herb Rogoff
Rockport, Massachusetts

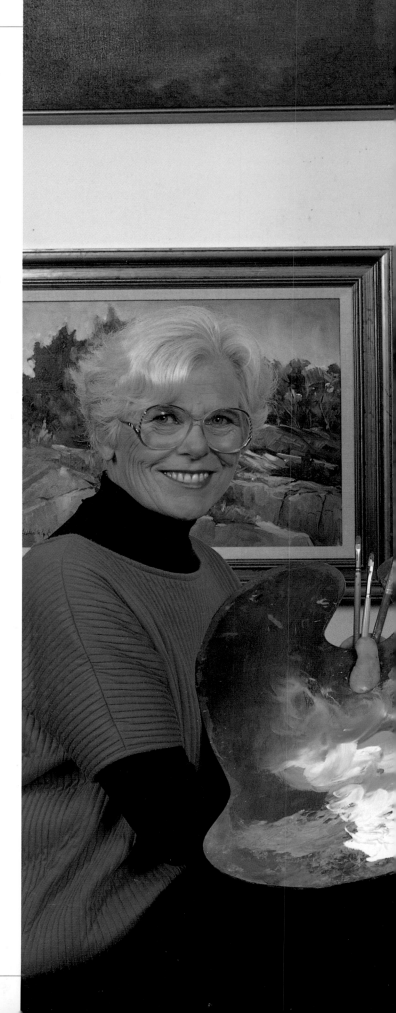

My Basic Palette

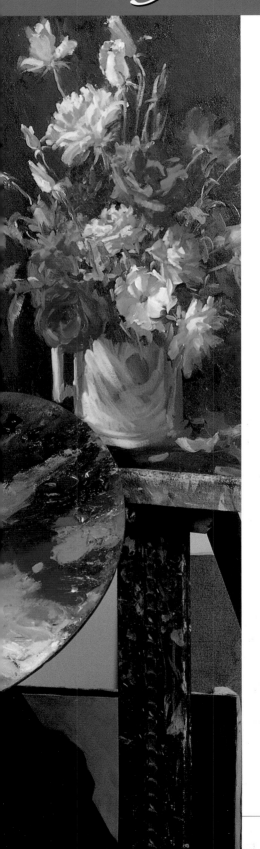

My basic palette is made up of six colors — yellow, orange, red (the warm ones), violet, blue, green (the cool ones). These six colors are divided into four groups:

The first group — the three warm colors in their light, bright form.

The second group — the three warm colors in a darker, duller form.

The third group — the three warm colors in their darkest, dullest form.

The fourth group — the three cool colors in a dark, intense form. These cool colors can be modified toward lightness or darkness and toward brightness or dullness by their mixture with black and white.

In addition to these colors, there is a lightening agent — white — at one extreme end and a darkening agent — black — at the other extreme.

With these colors on your palette you can arrive at any hue, tone or intensity you would need for any painting. I'm sure that you are aware that there are artists who believe in the theory that a painter needs only the three primary colors, along with black and white, to paint any picture. On the surface, this would seem to be correct, but it does not work as well in practice. Although these artists can mix the secondary colors from the primaries quite effortlessly, and, with black and white would seem to be able to create a range of tones, they get into trouble when they find they cannot easily mix the various intensities. This is why we have the three warm colors in three different intensities: light and brilliant, duller and darker, dullest and darkest. A perfect analogy that can make this concept understandable, is to compare the artist's palette to a symphony orchestra. After all, the aim in both forms is to create an artistic offering by utilizing every element. The string section of an orchestra, for example, can produce light tones (violins), darker tones (violas), still darker tones (cellos) and the darkest tones (bass viola or double bass). The same holds true in the wood-wind section: light — oboe; darker — clarinet; darkest — bassoon; extending also to the brass and percussion sections. This combination of instruments of various "intensities" creates an orchestra capable of interpreting the most well-rounded piece of music — a symphony. I hope you can now see the importance of having colors on your palette that can produce the wide range of intensities that representational painting demands.

Description and Uses of Colors

🌰 ZINC WHITE

White is the basis for all oil painting because it is used to lighten colors which, in their mass tones (as they come from the tube), are strong. As you know, white is not a color, but as a paint it is indispensable and versatile, and must be used, along with black, to get many of the different tones and intensities. Zinc White is the lightest in tone of all paint, is opaque and has great covering power. It is used more than black in getting gradations in tone. The light areas of a painting usually have a heavier and thicker paint layer than the dark areas because white has been used to lighten the tone of these areas and has brought its characteristic heaviness to these parts of the picture. Dark areas will have a thinner layer of paint because no white, or little white, has been used there.

As mentioned earlier, white is not a color, therefore it is impossible to paint anything with just white paint.

A good exercise would be to set up a still life of so-called white objects. Use a white cloth, a white egg and a white dish. Shine a light on this array of subject matter and you will see that none of the objects are pure white. Even if the cloth, the egg and the dish are absolutely white, color will appear because of the light that falls on them and from the reflections from other things in the room. Color is relative, of course, and when you are looking for color on white objects, don't expect to find it in vivid intensity.

One more word about the use of white: chalkiness is a condition that crops up when too much white paint or too much turpentine has been used. If your paintings lack a certain richness, it may be that you should have originally used light colors to create the light tones and steered away from so much white.

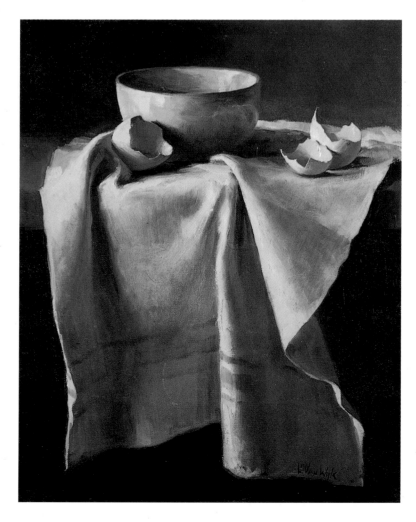

Study in White, 20 x 24", *Private Collection*
In this painting, even though all pure white objects are represented — the bowl, the eggshells and the cloth — you can see how different they become from each other because of the way they are affected by the light.

THALO YELLOW GREEN

A light yellow that's greenish in hue. Before it was developed under this name by Grumbacher, the manufacturer did not have a color to fill the gap between the Cadmium Yellows and Permanent Green Light. Thalo Yellow Green, with additions of white, creates yellow tints that neither Permanent Green Light nor Cadmium Yellow Light is capable of producing.

- It gets more and more yellow as it is mixed with greater amounts of white.
- It's excellent for sunlight shining on green grass.
- When mixed with Thalo Green or Ivory Black, it makes natural looking yellowish greens.
- Mixed with a violet (its complement), you can get beautiful flesh tones.

Using Thalo Yellow Green to Paint the Green of an Apple

This color is ideal for painting red apples with green spots. Here's how:

STEP 1. Paint in the Thalo Yellow Green, which is lighter and more delicate than the red that will be used next, making the shape larger than it will eventually be on the finished painting of the apple.

STEP 2. Using a lighter version of the red (Cadmium Red Light and white), begin the blend of Thalo Yellow Green into the red.

STEP 3. Using the actual red you want, which is Grumbacher Red and Alizarin Crimson, paint it into the intermediate red color of Step 2. You can use this technique whenever you want a dramatic change from one color to another. Step 2's use of the intermediate color is vitally important because it gives you a blend without creating a dirty passage.

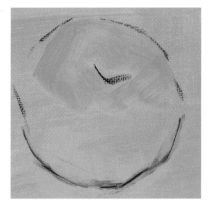 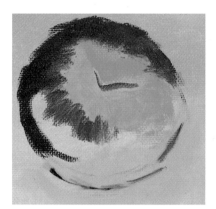 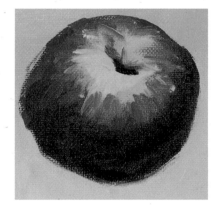

STEP 1.   **STEP 2.**   **STEP 3.**

CADMIUM YELLOW LIGHT

Cadmium Yellow comes in three tones: Cadmium Yellow Light, Cadmium Yellow Medium, Cadmium Yellow Deep. I use Cadmium Yellow Light as a staple on my palette; I use the medium version from time to time; rarely do I use the deep one. Cadmium Yellow Medium and Cadmium Yellow Deep contain some red in them which, if I need any, can be easily mixed by using Cadmium Yellow Light, which is a true yellow.

Cadmium Yellow Light is light in tone and bright in intensity, but I must alert you to the fact that it should be used sparingly in its pure form because it is never seen undiluted in large areas. Cadmium Yellow Light is used mainly for intermixing. In flower paintings, though, all the light, bright colors are used lavishly in unmixed form.

- It brightens and lightens green and mixes with blue to make various hues of green that are especially useful in landscape painting.
- It mixes with Burnt Umber to make a general hue for painting brass.
- It should never be used to paint a dark, dull object. It mixes well with the reds of the palette to create certain orange colors.
- It can be grayed down and made less intense by the addition of its complement, violet, a mixture of Alizarin Crimson and gray.
- When mixed with white it makes a good highlight for brass.
- It should never be mixed with black alone except when olive greens are desired.
- It can be darkened with Yellow Ochre or Raw Sienna and still maintain its yellow color.

Using Cadmium Yellow Light to Paint a Grapefruit

An example for the use of Cadmium Yellow Light is painting a grapefruit.

THE BODY TONE: Lighten the Cadmium Yellow Light with white or darken it with a darker yellow such as Yellow Ochre. If the grapefruit appears to be greenish, add a touch of green; if orange in hue, add some Cadmium Orange.

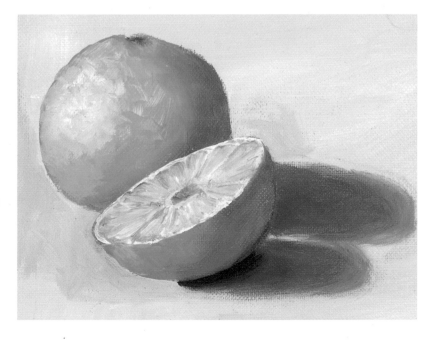

THE BODY SHADOW: A mixture of Cadmium Yellow Light and gray plus a little of Alizarin Crimson, the complement. This body shadow should match the shadow you see on the grapefruit and be in good tonal relation to the body tone. Inside the body shadow of the grapefruit there will be a yellow color caused by reflected light. This can be depicted with a darker yellow — Yellow Ochre — mixed with the shadow color.

THE CAST SHADOW: Paint the cast shadow in a grayed-down hue that is complementary to the object on which it is cast. Of course, the cast shadow will be darker than the surface on which it is seen. Students get more confused by cast shadows than by any other tone. It's easy if you keep in mind that the cast shadow is complementary to the object it is on not to the object casting it. If a shadow from a green vase is cast on a maple table, the cast shadow would be painted violet, the complement of the yellowish maple, instead of red which would be the complement of the object's green. After a cast shadow is painted in the complementary color in a dark, neutral form, paint inside this shadow some of the color of the surface on which the shadow is cast. In the case of the maple table, the yellow you have mixed for the table would be added back into the shadow in a darker tone to give it life and prevent it from looking like a plain, monotonous area. Since this method applies to all cast shadows, I will not repeat it in any of the instructions that follow in this section.

REFLECTIONS: With a mixture of Yellow Ochre and Cadmium Yellow Light add any reflections you see on the dark side of the grapefruit. If some nearby object is reflecting its color — maybe a blue or green — then that color would also appear in the reflection, greatly reduced in intensity, of course.

HIGHLIGHTS: Last of all you will have to paint the highlight, which is in direct line with the light. In the case of a yellow grapefruit, the highlight would be made of a lot of white with the merest hint of Alizarin Crimson, yellow's complement.

🌿 CADMIUM ORANGE

Cadmium Orange is light in tone and bright in intensity and can, if necessary, be substituted by Cadmium Yellow Deep.

• It will make hues of dull green when mixed with blue or black.

• It will lighten Thalo Green and at the same time diminish its intensity (this happens because the red in the orange neutralizes green).

• It will brighten reds and Burnt Sienna.

• In its pure form it is used even less frequently than Cadmium Yellow Light but is good in unmixed form for painting fruits and flowers.

• It can be neutralized by intermixing with gray or its complement, a grayed-down blue. (If the blue is not grayed-down, the mixture of it and the orange may make a green.)

• If mixed with lots of white, it is good for painting clouds.

Using Cadmium Orange to Paint a Tangerine

A tangerine has a characteristic shape: it is flatter on top and is dimpled at the stem end. These features, plus the thinner skin, make it different from the orange.

THE BODY TONE: Should be painted with a mixture of Cadmium Orange, white, and a touch of Burnt Sienna. This mixture will only guide you to find the correct tone; your judgment and your eye will be the final authority as to the quantity of each color in the mixture to make it match the fruit that's your model.

THE BODY SHADOW: Use some of the body mixture plus a little Cobalt Blue or Thalo Blue (complements) and mix with dark gray.

REFLECTIONS: Can be represented with Cadmium Orange plus Burnt Sienna painted in the body shadow.

HIGHLIGHT: Calls for white barely tinted with the complement of the orange — blue.

You may add interest by opening the fruit and exposing sections of it, as shown in the illustration. Paint the pulp with Cadmium Orange and Cadmium Yellow Light with a bit of white; the darker areas with Cadmium Orange with a bit of Burnt Sienna. Where light shines through a section — its translucency — use Cadmium Orange, Cadmium Yellow Light and white.

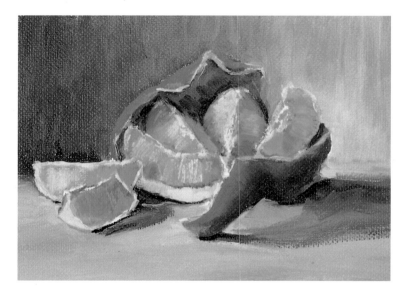

🌿 CADMIUM RED LIGHT

Cadmium Red Light is light in tone and bright in intensity. It is used more often than Cadmium Orange because it can be used as an orange as well as a red. When used as a red, its complement is, of course, green; as an orange it has blue as the complement. Cadmium Red Light can be substituted by the prohibitively priced Vermilion.

• It varies considerably according to each manufacturer's formula. Grumbacher's is quite orange; Winsor & Newton's less so. Make your own test with other manufacturers' versions by tinting each one with white .

• It makes a good flesh color when mixed with Yellow Ochre and white.

- It makes pink for flower painting when mixed with white.
- It should not be used when making a dark, dull red.
- It is useful in making copper tones.
- It can be darkened in tone and lessened in intensity by the addition of Light Red.
- It can be lightened in tone without loss of intensity by the addition of Cadmium Orange.
- It is too intense to use undiluted in large areas.
- It should never be used unmixed in a background.

Using Cadmium Red Light to Paint Plum Tomatoes

The popularity of Italian food in our daily fare has given the still life painter additional subject matter to use in paintings: dried spaghetti, garlics, red peppers, cheese and plum tomatoes, which are so important in making a good sauce.

THE BODY TONE: Cadmium Red Light, Alizarin Crimson and a little white, mixed until you get a hue that's representative of tomatoes.

THE BODY SHADOW: Must be darker than the body tone, so add some of the complement (green) to the body tone and some Alizarin Crimson or black to make it dark enough.

REFLECTIONS: Into the body tone color mix a little of the color which is reflecting. If the tomato is resting on a white cloth, add a little white to the body tone to represent the reflections the cloth is making on the shadowed side.

HIGHLIGHT: Made of white and the tiniest speck of the complement green.

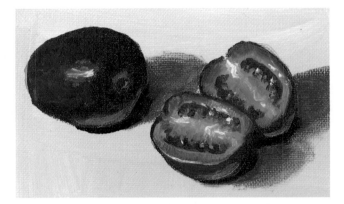

🍎 GRUMBACHER RED

Grumbacher Red, and similar reds made by other manufacturers, is a bright, medium-toned red that veers neither toward orange nor blue as other reds tend to do. It can surely be labeled as a neutral red, which becomes evident when you mix amounts of white into it.

- It is a neutral red that is permanent.
- It can withstand admixtures of lots of white without losing its "pure red" characteristic.
- It's important in flesh mixtures with yellow and white.
- It makes a lovely gray when mixed with Chromium Oxide Green and black and white.
- It becomes a darker, rich red when mixed with Alizarin Crimson.
- It can be used as a spectrum red.
- When painting the color of Old Glory or just plain apples, you can't do without Grumbacher Red.

Using Grumbacher Red to Paint a Red Pepper

THE BODY TONE: Mix Grumbacher Red into a gray of black and white.

THE BODY SHADOW: Add Alizarin Crimson in the body tone mixture.

WHERE THE LIGHT STRIKES: To the body tone mixture, add a small amount of Cadmium Red Light.

HIGHLIGHT: White with a slight touch of Viridian.

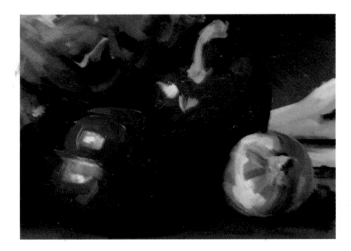

YELLOW OCHRE

Yellow Ochre is a yellow in a medium tone and medium intensity and is a color that is often found in nature. Its lower intensity and tone duplicate countless objects. It is a color that can't be made or mixed easily. Here are some distinct characteristics of this darker, duller yellow:

- It's lightened in tone quickly when mixed with white because it is a weaker pigment.
- It's grayed by the addition of yellow's complement, violet (Alizarin Crimson mixed with gray).
- It turns green when mixed with black.
- It makes a lighter, brighter green hue when mixed with Thalo Green.
- Mixed with Cadmium Red Light it makes a good skin color.
- Mixed with white and Light Red it makes a duller skin tone.
- Mixed with white and Alizarin Crimson it makes a skin color for painting a person with violet hues in the skin.

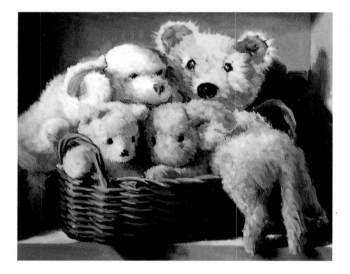

Using Yellow Ochre to Paint a Wicker Basket

Since wicker is near Yellow Ochre in tone and hue, you can learn some of the characteristics of Yellow Ochre by painting a wicker basket.

THE BODY TONE: Yellow Ochre mixed with Burnt Umber and white.

THE BODY SHADOW: Use the body tone mixture plus some complementary Alizarin Crimson, for neutralizing effect, and black to make it dark enough.

THE CAST SHADOW: This is complementary to the color of the surface it falls on. In this picture, the shadow falls on the Yellow Ochre frame that's part of the painting. The color of the cast shadow, therefore, should be some form of violet (Alizarin Crimson which has been darkened).

REFLECTIONS: Pure Yellow Ochre in the body shadow.

HIGHLIGHT: Since this type of material absorbs light more than it reflects it, there are no real highlights. If, however, you add white to Yellow Ochre, making it lighter in tone than the body tone mixture, the weave of the basket can be emphasized where light hits the high spots of the texture. If shiny spots seem to be seen on the basket, indicate this with some white mixed with very little Alizarin Crimson, the complement of yellow.

Flash's Toys, 14 x 18", *Private Collection*
My little black whippet, Flash, loved to play with her stuffed bears and, miraculously, never damaged any of them. I stored them in this wicker basket and in tribute to Flash, who died that summer, I painted it as my last demonstration for the season.

RAW SIENNA

Raw Sienna is an orange of medium tone and intensity and is used whenever an object has a body tone that resembles gold. Raw Sienna plus its complement, blue, is valuable for painting the shadowed side of anything in the yellow family.

- It can be brightened with Cadmium Yellow Light or Cadmium Orange.
- Mixed with black, it turns olive green which you'll find useful for landscapes and for adding to flesh tones for the shadowed parts of the face.
- It is a good color for painting brass.

Raw Sienna (cont.)

- It is an orange which is yellow in hue, so you will find that violet is sometimes successfully used as its complement.
- It is similar to Yellow Ochre in many respects and the hints that you'll find under Yellow Ochre will apply here.

Using Raw Sienna to Paint a Gilt-Edged Book

Using down strokes, paint the side planes of the book's pages: the light side, the dark side.

With a mixture of Raw Sienna, Yellow Ochre and a little white, paint the side plane that faces the light. The highlight is white, a touch of Yellow Ochre and some

Cadmium Yellow Light. Make the highlight with a stroke that's opposite to the downward stroke.

On the shadowed side of these edges the tones darker than they are on the light side, The darker tone made by adding Ivory Black and Alizarin Crimson to the mass tone.

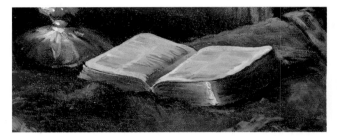

🍂 LIGHT RED

Light Red is a color of medium tone and intensity and, because of its name, is often confused with Cadmium Red Light, which, as everyone knows, is light and bright, making it entirely different. Light Red is also known as English Red Light and some manufacturers carry both names on their labels. If you have Terra Rosa or Venetian Red in your paint box, they can be used as reliable substitutes for Light Red. Here are some characteristics of this darker, duller red:

- It makes a good pink when diluted with white.
- It makes a brilliant, dark red when mixed with Alizarin Crimson.
- It's useful in portrait painting for adding rosy hues to highly colored areas.

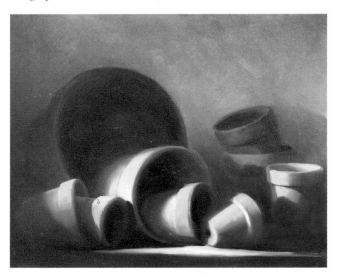

- It can be neutralized by the addition of green, its complement.
- It can be darkened and still keep its red hue by the addition of Burnt Umber.

Using Light Red to Paint Clay Pots

THE BODY TONE: Light Red with a small amount of gray.

THE BODY SHADOW: Darken the puddle of body tone mixture with its complement, green, and if it needs further darkening, add a little Ivory Black.

CAST SHADOW: The cast shadows are those that fall from one pot onto another. The color of these cast shadows would be green that has been grayed quite a bit with black and white. Very little table shows since the view of the pots is head on rather than looking down at them. Consequently, there are no discernible cast shadows on the table top.

REFLECTIONS: There will be few reflections and highlights in these objects since they are rough and absorbent. The varying light tones on the light sides are made by mixing Light Red, Yellow Ochre and white. The few reflections you can find should be painted with plain Light Red.

Waiting for LIfe, 20 x 24", *Private Collection*
I'd seen this arrangement many times at the local nursery and I'm sure many of you have, too. I decided to paint these various-sized clay pots, which I very carefully set up to look as though they had been randomly scattered about just waiting for soil and seed.

🍂 BURNT UMBER

Burnt Umber is yellow in the darkest, dullest form. I consider it to be the most indispensable color on my palette. There are so many things that are of tones of this dark, dull yellow that we can say that we live not in a green world but in one of Burnt Umber. Many of you may find it hard to think of this color as a yellow, but you must classify it as such to keep an orderly mind about colors and complements.

• It can be made into a lighter, orange-yellow hue by adding Burnt Sienna.

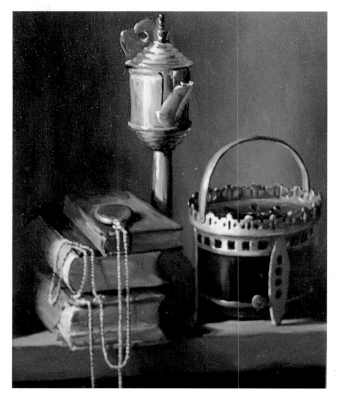

• It can be made into a dark, orange hue by adding Alizarin Crimson.

• Most things in the tan or beige family are Burnt Umber and white.

• It is a neutral yellow but can be further neutralized by intermixing with gray.

Using Burnt Umber to Paint a Brass Object

The subject in this painting is an old, Dutch oil lamp. The instructions for painting it can apply to any brass object, such as the tea warmer that's seen on the right.

THE BODY TONE: Burnt Umber and Cadmium Yellow Light.

THE BODY SHADOW: Add violet (Alizarin Crimson and black) to this mixture. If the body shadow seems to need more darks, add some blue.

THE CAST SHADOW: Since there are none visible on the table, the shadows that are cast in various areas of the oil lamp should be painted in a violet that's a bit darker than the body shadow.

REFLECTIONS: Use pure Burnt Umber to put in the reflections that you see on the shadow side.

HIGHLIGHT: The highlight on brass is an exception to the rule; it is not complementary in color to the object it is on. Instead, make the highlight a light, bright mixture of Cadmium Yellow Light and white

A Dutch Still Life, 12 x 16", *Private Collection*
The two brass objects in this composition are treated exactly alike.

🍂 BURNT SIENNA

Burnt Sienna is a dark, dull orange that is used almost as much as Burnt Umber.

• It is a strong pigment, so use it sparingly.

• It is made into a glowing, golden beige by adding white.

• It is made into a shiny gold by mixing with Cadmium Yellow Light.

• It is added to gray for use on the shadowed side of the face and neck when painting portraits.

• It is a splendid paint for backgrounds when intermixed.

• It will accentuate the red quality of Alizarin Crimson, the reason being that Alizarin Crimson contains both red and blue making a violet. When Burnt Sienna, an orange, is added to Alizarin Crimson, the orange minimizes the complementary blue contained in the Alizarin Crimson.

For instructions on the use of Burnt Sienna, please refer to "Copper Tray" on page 35 in the Color Recipes section.

ALIZARIN CRIMSON

Alizarin Crimson is an old standby on almost every painter's palette. It is valuable in itself and as an admixture. Although the word "crimson" may call up visions of red, Alizarin Crimson is not a primary red, as an army of beginners must have discovered the first time they mixed it with white. Alizarin Crimson is classified as a violet because it turns violet when mixed with black, blue, gray or white. If unmixed with white or any opaque color, it is very transparent, making it invaluable for glazing.

• When mixed with any other red, it has green as its complement; when used as violet, its complement is yellow.

• It becomes a pleasing red orange when mixed with Cadmium Yellow Light. Blue is its complement.

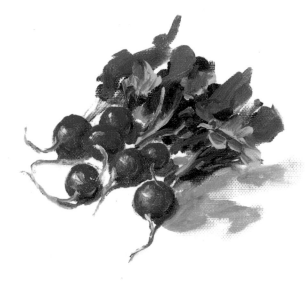

• It makes a light, bright red when mixed with Cadmium Orange, with green as the complement.

• It makes a perfect violet when mixed with gray for painting the dark side of such yellow objects as lemons, squash and bananas.

• It makes a light-toned violet when mixed with white.

• It mixes well with black, creating a rich, dark red violet.

• It mixes with Indian Red to form an intense red of medium tone.

• It makes the darkest possible orange when mixed with Burnt Umber. In this instance the Alizarin Crimson is the dark red and the Burnt Umber is the dark yellow thus creating a dark orange.

• It makes a cool gray when mixed with green and gray.

Using Alizarin Crimson to Paint Radishes

THE BODY TONE: Alizarin Crimson and gray made of Ivory Black and white.

THE BODY SHADOW: Add Alizarin Crimson and just a touch of Viridian.

ON THE LIGHT SIDE: Add a little Cadmium Red Light to Grumbacher Red.

REFLECTIONS: Add a little more white to the body tone color and paint it into the edge of the shadow.

HIGHLIGHT: White with a mere touch of Viridian.

THALO BLUE

Thalo Blue is dark in tone and strong in intensity. It is so very intense, in fact, that one must usually lighten it and dull it. It is both lightened and brightened when white is added, as are all the cool colors. It is dulled by the addition of gray. All cool colors can be controlled in tone and intensity with gray (made of black and white).

• It makes a light, bright blue when mixed with white.

• It makes all hues of green by intermixing with different yellows. The hue of the green depends upon the yellow

that is used and the amount of it. Practice is needed to learn what greens will result when Thalo Blue is mixed with the following yellows: Cadmium Yellow Light, Yellow Ochre and Burnt Umber.

• Even though it is already dark, it can be mixed with black.

• It makes a pleasing and useful cool background color when mixed with lots of gray or with its complement orange.

• Since it is such a strong pigment, it should be squeezed onto the palette sparingly.

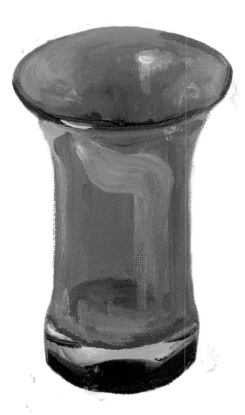

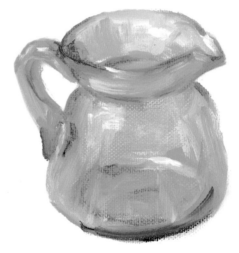

Using Thalo Blue to Paint a Blue Vase

THE BODY TONE: Thalo Blue and gray made of Ivory Black and white.

THE BODY SHADOW: Thalo Blue and Alizarin Crimson were added to the previous step.

THE LIGHTER LIGHTS: Thalo Blue and white.

THE HAZE: Add more white to the body tone.

HIGHLIGHT: White with a bit of Cadmium Orange.

THALO GREEN

Thalo Green is a blue green of dark tone and strong intensity.

• It usually has to be dulled with black and white because it is too intense to use pure.

• It can be lightened with white.

• It can be lightened and brightened by adding bright yellows.

• It can be made more yellow in hue by mixing with Cadmium Yellow Light, Yellow Ochre or Raw Sienna.

• It mixes with gray to make a useful, neutral blue green.

• It can be neutralized by the addition of its complement red. Any red mixes well with it.

• Mixed with Alizarin Crimson, it makes black.

Using Thalo Green to Paint a Green Pitcher

THE BODY TONE: Thalo Green into a gray made of Ivory Black and white and just a bit of Alizarin Crimson.

THE BODY SHADOW: To the body tone, add Thalo Green, Ivory Black and Alizarin Crimson.

THE LIGHTER LIGHTS: Thalo Green and Thalo Yellow Green.

THE HAZE: Add Ivory Black and white to a very bit of Alizarin Crimson.

THE HIGHLIGHT: White and a mere touch of Alizarin Crimson.

REFLECTION: Much darker version of the body tone but not as dark as the body shadow.

IVORY BLACK

Ivory Black is the black that's most compatible with the colors of my palette. It is a transparent, true black and does not muddy colors. Black, like white, is not a color. And like white, it should never be used pure but always as part of a mixture.

A gray made with black, white and either a warm or cool color is the basis of all the mixtures. The neutrality of gray makes it complementary to all colors. This is a good thing to remember. A gray area becomes complementary to any color placed next to it. Our eye makes it complementary because we always need to see the three primary colors.

Some artists recoil at the mere mention of black paint. Students who have been taught to regard black as a sort of poison are hard to convince that black is nothing to fear and is necessary for controlling the tones of colors. The despisers of black do not have black on their palettes but when they must have a dark tone value, they either use dark gray, which contains black, or a color and its complement in their darkest value and so, in the process, they actually create black. Black always results from mixing a dark color and its dark complement. If these artists had black on their palettes, they could darken their colors with it very easily and quickly, saving all the time it takes to make a dark neutral tone without using black. They could also darken colors without graying them as the complement does.

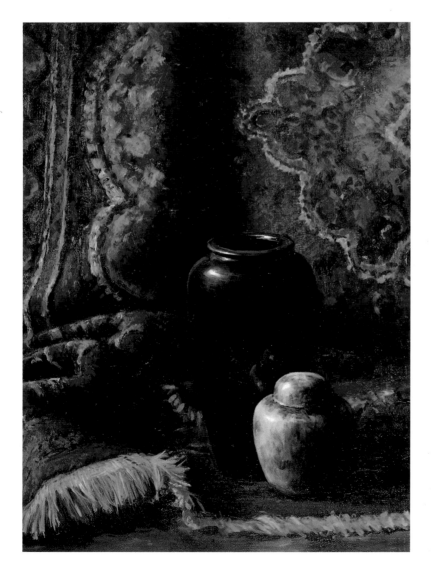

Dutch Table Cover, 20 x 24", *Private Collection*
I have painted the black vase many times before but never in an obviously Dutch setting. Every household in Holland, it seems, owns a cover like the one shown, in various designs, of course. With a Dutch ginger pot also in the composition, the black vase becomes alien to the theme of Holland things. But it all works, proving that not every item in a still life has to conform to the main idea of the painting.

The Color Recipes

The *Color Recipes* have been designed to read like a cookbook. What makes a *Color Recipe* different from a cookbook recipe, you will find, is that I do not provide you with the *amount* of color you should use for each item you are painting; I am leaving that to you for your own experimentation. But I *do*, of course, mention the color names, which are mainly the ones I've just discussed in the section, *My Basic Palette*. I suggest that you check your paint box for these colors, filling in those you don't have.

I use some other colors that are not part of my basic palette. From time to time these colors are mentioned in the *Recipes*. These are the extras useful for certain subject matter. Here, again, I suggest that you check your paint box to see whether or not you have these colors, just as you would check your cooking supplies before starting to cook. I'm sure all of you would never read the ingredients you'd need for a cooking recipe while you are actually at the stove. By the same token, you can't be at your easel with your brush in hand before knowing whether or not you have all the colors you'd need.

In order to make this process easier for you, I have listed below all of the extra colors that show up in the *Recipes* in this book. Add this list to the colors of my basic palette, and check against your supply of colors. Here, then, are the extra colors:

Red — Indian Red, Venetian Red

Yellow — Cadmium Yellow Medium

Blue — Cerulean Blue, Cobalt Blue, Payne's Gray, Ultramarine Blue

Green — Chromium Oxide Green, Sap Green, Viridian

Earth Color — Raw Umber

Violet — Manganese Violet, Thalo Red Rose

The *Color Recipes* in this book, as well as in the first one we've published, are unique. They can be used as a course of study or they can be used just as a reference. We must point out that when working with a *Recipe*, you will want to have the actual subject to look at so the visual experience can add that personal touch.

Babbling Brooks

A very difficult subject. The biggest mistake — using pure white, very thickly applied, to represent the water's agitation. An application of *thick* paint bears no resemblance to the *fluid* quality of water.

How do you avoid this? Make a mixture of white, Cerulean Blue, and Burnt Umber (more toward blue than toward brown). Make this tone about #3 if #1 is white and #10 is black on a value scale.

1. Paint this color wherever you see water. Into this mixture, add darker tones to represent any rocks you see in the water, and add more Burnt Umber into this mixture with a little Ultramarine Blue or Ivory Black for any shadows.

2. Lighten this basic mixture with white and Cerulean Blue and work this mixture in to represent the areas that look to be the lightest tones in the water.

3. Now add more white into the mixture with a little bit of Yellow Ochre, and paint in the very lightest areas.

You can see that this is a process of starting darker and gradually lightening. The agitation of the water, as a result, will become part of the entire body of water.

When painting waterfalls, apply the basic tone on opposite from the way the water is falling. Then, you can stroke lighter tones in the direction of the falling water.

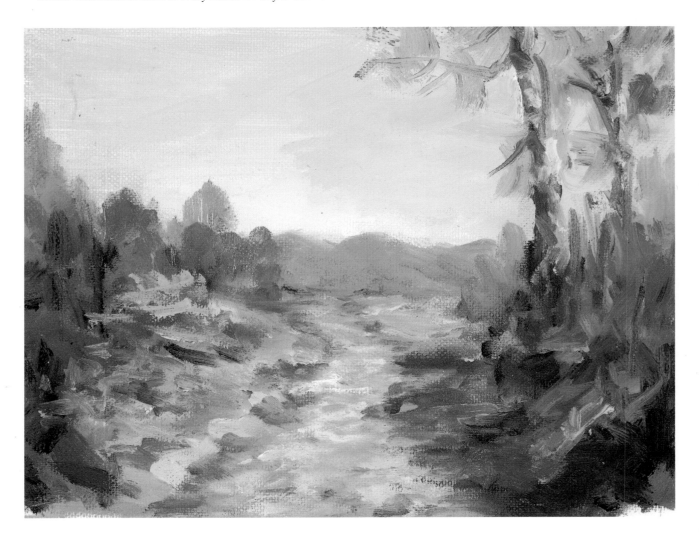

Lakes

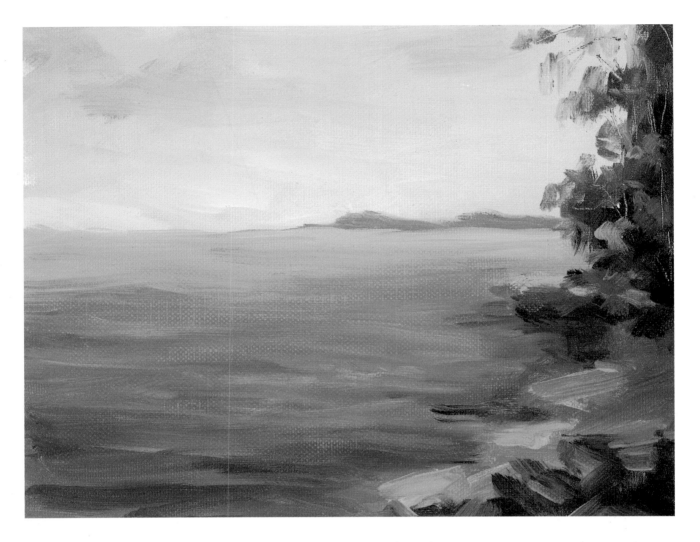

The color of any body of water is directly related to the color of the sky. The brighter the sky, the brighter the color of the water; the more overcast, the duller the water. The biggest mistake I've seen in paintings of water is the painter allowing his color to get uncontrollably brilliant. Here's how to avoid this:

1. Mass your water area in with the color you've used for the sky, adding a little Burnt Umber and Thalo Blue in it to dull it.

2. Paint into this with jabs of all the colors you see in the areas that surround the water and which will also affect the water.

3. Now your painted area could be called bluish in color. It could be considered cool. Mix white, Payne's Gray and Burnt Umber to make a warm gray. Skim over the painted area to give the effect of light striking the water.

4. Most often the color of the lake is light when it's farther away and darker when it's closer to you. It may not appear that way when you look at it, but by painting it in this manner, you'll increase the feeling of depth in your picture.

Snow on Mountains

Who can resist the temptation to paint the snow of the Rockies? Since we rarely see the entire mountain covered with snow, the problem is to paint the area where the snow-line meets the bare portions of the mountain.

1. Make sure the patch of snow is an interesting and convincing shape in relation to the mountain. Paint it a tone of warm gray that makes it seem that it's on a correct distance plane. If this tone of gray is too light, it will come forward, off the mountain. It's better to start the snow too dark — you can always lighten it.

2. Here's a good mixture for snow on mountains: a gray made of Cobalt Blue and Burnt Sienna mixed into white. Make this gray more warm if the sun's striking the mountain by using more Burnt Sienna. Make it cooler if the snow's in shadow by using more Cobalt Blue.

3. Often we see shadows on the snow on mountains caused by jutting rocks. These shadows lend a lot of interest to the snow patch. Make these shadows by putting Ultramarine Blue and a little Alizarin Crimson into the gray.

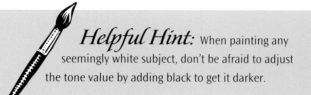

Helpful Hint: When painting any seemingly white subject, don't be afraid to adjust the tone value by adding black to get it darker.

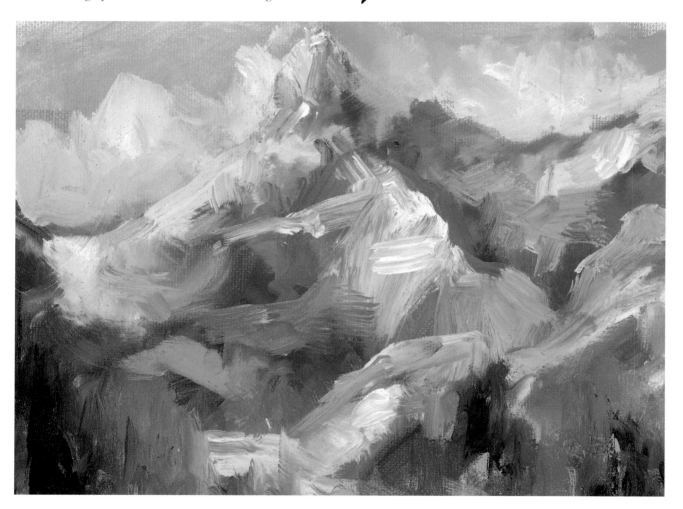

Snow in Shadow

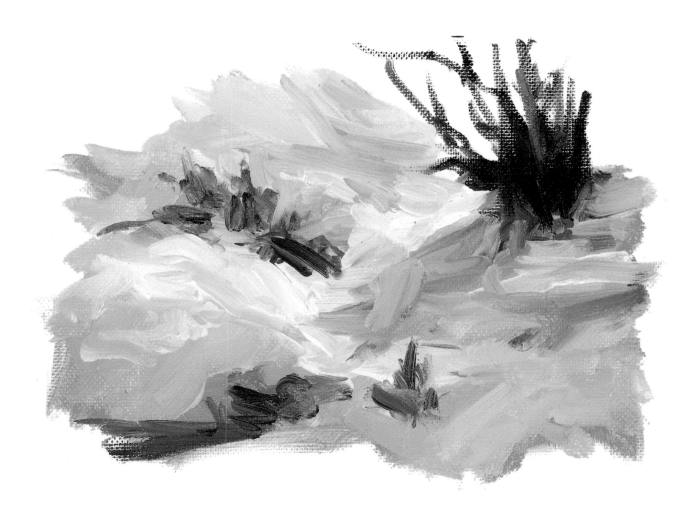

Herewith, some basic gray-blue mixtures for shadows on snow:

1. White, Cerulean Blue, and a little Burnt Umber.

2. White, Cobalt Blue, a touch of Alizarin Crimson, and Raw Umber.

3. Ivory Black, white, a touch of Thalo Blue, Thalo Red Rose, and a little Yellow Ochre.

Use any one of these mixtures to paint in the pattern of your shadows. Now, add a little bit of white and Yellow Ochre or Raw Sienna or Burnt Umber or Thalo Yellow Green into the gray-blue, and paint this slightly warmer gray into your already painted shadows, leaving the original gray-blue more on the edge of the shadows.

This two-step operation makes the paint interpret the shadows more convincingly, because there's always some degree of reflected light in both body shadows and cast shadows.

Snow on a Sunny Day

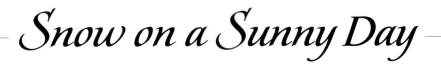

1. Sun brings out a lot of color. To paint the sparkle of snow on a sunny day, mass the snow area in with white and an itsy-bitsy amount of Alizarin Crimson, and even itsier-bitsier Ivory Black.

2. Take a big glob of white and add it into a little bit of Cadmium Yellow Medium and drag this warm, light white over the already painted areas.

3. Of course, the shadows on the snow will be violet or blue (complement of sunlit snow). These shadow colors could be:
   Ivory Black, white, Alizarin Crimson, a little Thalo Blue.
   or Ivory Black, white, Cobalt Blue, a little Burnt Umber
   or Ivory Black, white, Ultramarine Blue.

4. If you feel there are a few areas that you want to be very very light, you can take white with a breath of Alizarin Crimson and drag this color over the snow.

Helpful Hint: Make sure your snow color is grayed and darkened in the distance. You get this by using a darker gray (more Ivory Black) with these colors.

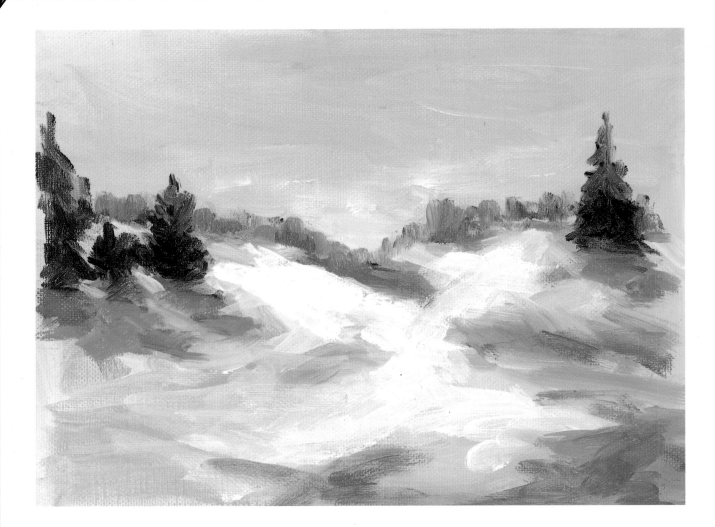

Stormy Skies

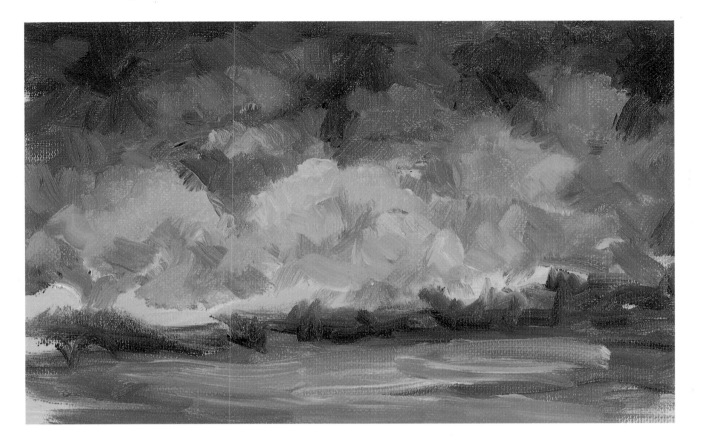

The most common cause of unconvincing-looking subject matter in landscape paintings can be traced back to the painters' obsessions with pre-conceived ideas of what something looks like instead of recording the true effects of nature's moods.

I've said this many times before, and I'll say it again: graying the color with the color's complement — or mixing the color into gray instead of into white — will give a more luminous feeling to your paintings, no matter what object it is that you're painting. Now, let's put this into practice:

A successful way to paint the blue of a stormy sky is to have a dark gray ominous cloud pattern in contrast to a very light warm gray patch of clear sky. Strangely enough, the clear sky isn't blue, it's silvery looking. Get this by mixing Ivory Black and white and Burnt Umber; or white, Indian Red, and a mere breath of Viridian.

The cloud becomes the cool color and is a darker gray plus Payne's Gray. Or it's Ultramarine Blue with a little Burnt Sienna into a darker gray.

If the light clear sky is off in the distance, and the dark cloud takes up the upper part of the canvas, it gives the appearance of the storm closing in. In fact, when painting any skies, don't ever make extreme light portions near the top of the canvas.

Another way to paint a stormy sky is to paint the whole sky area in a mixture of Ivory Black, white, and Burnt Sienna (light, warm gray). Then add into the painted area many versions of blue-gray, such as: Ultramarine Blue and Alizarin Crimson; or gray with some Viridian; or gray with Payne's Gray. The first layer of color should peek through in spots to give the mottled look of stormy skies.

Helpful Hint: When painting many kinds of sky effects, you must remove from your mind any idea that the sky is blue. There are literally thousands of paintings around with artificial looking skies because they are too blue.

Brilliant Red Sunset

Although a sunset is a very inspiring sight it doesn't lend itself easily to an inspiring painting. Why? One of the roles of a painting is to uplift the ordinary. A painting's source of inspiration isn't what you paint but how you paint it. As a result, a beautiful paint rendition and interpretation of green peppers, for example, can even charm a person who doesn't care for green peppers. Now, have you ever met anyone who doesn't care for sunsets?

If you must paint the setting sun, don't, for heaven's sake, work from picture postcards. Take your own color photographs and organize your compositions from them.

The setting sun is most spectacular when there's a fair amount of clouds. In this case you get the opportunity to have very light patches that can only appear that way simply because they contrast the dark clouds.

The most common mistake I've seen is making light areas that aren't saturated with enough white. The warm light colors, from orange to red violet, look raw and unilluminated. Make sure you mix the warm colors of the sunset into a good deal of white. These colors are:

Cadmium Orange into a lot of white / Thalo Red Rose into a lot of white / Cadmium Red Light into a lot of white The dark clouds that show these bright spots up are made of: white, Ivory Black, Burnt Umber, and Thalo Red Rose.

Helpful Hint: Paint your light areas in bigger than what they are, and then cut them down with the darker clouds.

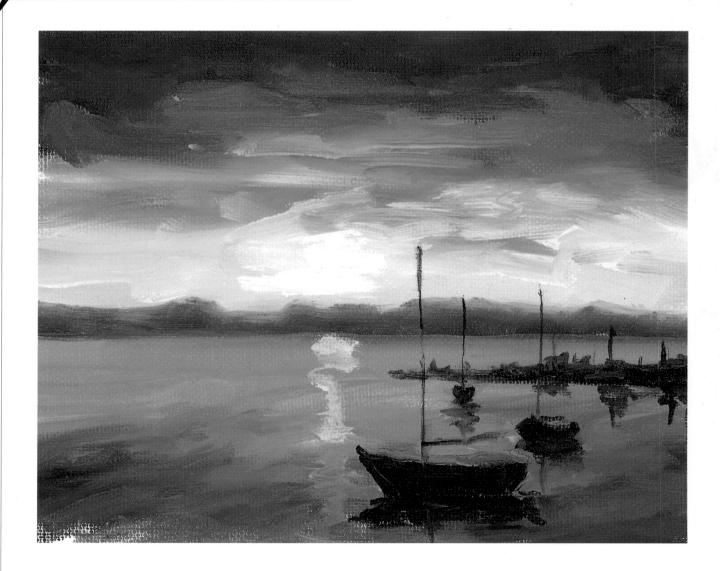

Moonlight

Painting moonlight can be considered a special effect. There are other moods like it in nature, and many of them break the general rules in painting. One of them is moonlight on the water. In this case the water's lighter than the sky. You'll also see this effect on cloudy days towards dusk.

You can imagine how tempting these special effects are to paint, because they do make dramatic pictures. Tempting, yes, but, oh, how difficult!

REMEMBER: You can't break the rules until you first know and understand them. Save the dramatic pictures for that time when you have accumulated some painting experience and more common effects. Once you learn the ordinary factors in nature and are aware of nature's secrets, use this knowledge to be more daring. So — here's how to paint a picture of moonlight:

Moonlight is very silvery and can be pictorialized by adding light accents of light warm gray (Ivory Black, white, Burnt Umber and a slight touch of Thalo Blue) to all things that the moonlight shines on. Remember, you can't show a light effect without having darkness to show it up. I can't stress enough that any light, whether from the moon, the sun or from a spotlight, shines in one direction, so all things that are in direct line with the light can be light because of the illumination.

Now, for all the colors that are seen in shadow: They have to be darkened with a dark warm gray made by mixing Burnt Umber and Thalo Blue into the color of each object. For example — this mixture into Venetian Red for a red barn, or this mixture into white for a white house, or this mixture into green for grass and trees. And so on.

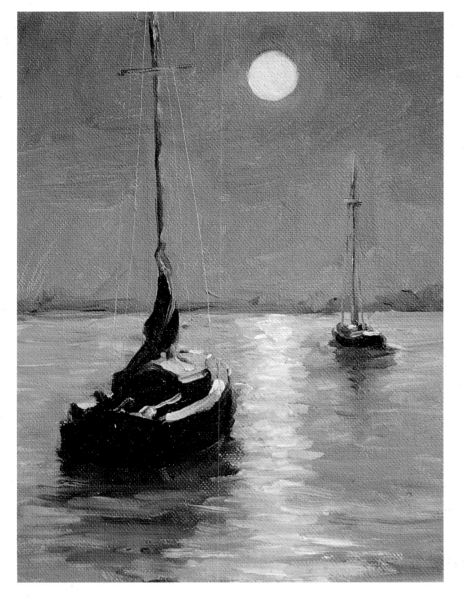

Remember, you can't show a light effect without having darkness to show it up.

Cumulus Clouds in a Bright Sky

Most common in Autumn, this sky effect can be the exciting factor that a quiet pastoral landscape needs. When doing this kind of sky, make sure you have the sky area large so that it becomes a strong part of the composition.

START WITH THE COLOR OF THE SKY: Way off in the distance where the sky meets the horizon, the mixture is white with Thalo Green.

For the more bluish color that you find when the sky comes forward towards you, add Cerulean Blue to the first mixture. As the sky color meets the top of the canvas, add Cobalt Blue to that mixture. If the mixture seems too bright, add a little bit of Burnt Umber to it.

CLOUD COLOR: For the mass tone of the cloud — Ivory Black, white, Burnt Umber and a touch of Yellow Ochre. This mixture should be a value that's just a little bit lighter than the sky color.

SHADOWS ON THE CLOUDS: Add a touch of Payne's Gray to this mixture.

WHERE THE LIGHT STRIKES THE CLOUDS: Where the light strikes the clouds — use white with a touch of of Payne's Gray. Or white with a touch of Ivory Black in it.

PROGRESSION OF APPLICATION: Make a drawing of the area that will be clouds and the area that will be sky. Paint in the sky color and work up towards the top of the canvas using the mixtures just given. Overlap your sky color into the area where the clouds will be. Don't be afraid to use a nice thick mixture, because your clouds will also be thickly painted. The entire sky should have the same thickness of application.

With a paint rag (preferably Turkish towling) wipe the blue away from where you slopped it into the cloud areas. Then, paint in the mass color of the cloud, fuzzing this color a bit into your sky color. Make your clouds take on a more definite form with your lighter colors and your shadow colors.

Helpful Hint: Make sure you start with the white, then put in a little Thalo Green and then, mix it quickly.

Beach Sand

Because beach sand is very light, its color is mistakenly thought of as Cadmium Yellow and white. There's a strong tendency to dip into the light colors of the palette when seeing very light tone values; a color, though, should be lightened with white.

Beach sand is very light; you've got to use a lot of white. Don't use a light yellow like Cadmium Yellow Light. Use, instead, a more muted yellow to get the yellow color. Some of these yellows are: Yellow Ochre, Burnt Umber, Raw Sienna, or Raw Umber.

1. As with so many other things in painting, start the beach sand a little darker than you see it. Use this mixture: Ivory Black and white and Alizarin Crimson to make a light gray-violet. Add into it a little Yellow Ochre and Burnt Umber to make the color of the sand where no sunlight strikes, such as the color you'd see in a footstep.

2. Now — using lots of white, Burnt Umber, and Yellow Ochre, work into this and try to make the rhythm of your strokes feel the texture of the sand.

3. If the sand is extremely bleached by the sun, take a lot of white with the merest touch of Yellow Ochre in it, and impart this lightest tone value by dragging it over your already painted area with a dry brush.

4. Any shadows that fall on the sand can be made by putting some Indian Red and a little Cobalt Blue into the original mass tone color.

How to Make Beach Sand Wet:

This poses quite a problem. Most often the tone of the wet sand is darker than the dry sand, and is quite reflective of its surroundings. It often reflects the color of the sky. To differentiate between wet and dry sand is to paint the wet sand with up-and-down brushstrokes and to paint the dry sand with across strokes. Up-and-down strokes are always an easier way to show a reflective surface .

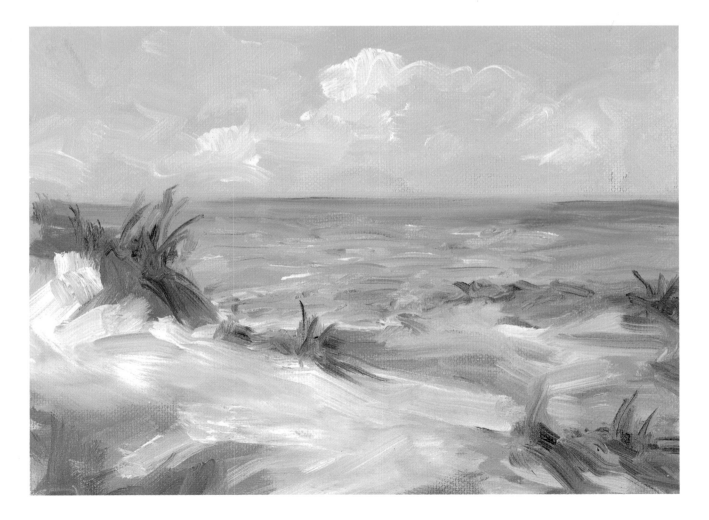

White Houses on a Sunny Day

The sun striking a white house among some trees or near a road is an appealing subject in landscape. Make sure you pick the view that shows two planes of the house with the sun striking only one of them.

THE SUNLIT SIDE OF THE HOUSE: should be massed in with white and a little Yellow Ochre. *IMPORTANT:* A light mixture will look more vital if you mix a lot more than you'll need, then don't mix it too much. *Here's how to do it:* move a gob of white with your brush to a mixing area on your palette. Touch your brush into the Yellow Ochre, then swirl it into the white. *Don't grind it in!* Now, pick up quite an amount of this mixture and lay the paint on the canvas.

THE SHADOW SIDE OF THE HOUSE: should be massed in with a darker value than the light side. Make this with Ivory Black and white and Alizarin Crimson. If this violet seems too harsh, add a touch of Raw Sienna. If the shadow looks more blue, add Cerulean Blue.

FOR ANY CAST SHADOWS: from trees or the overhang of the roof on the sunlit side, use the same violet mixture that you used on the shadow side.

If the shadowed side of the house is big enough, it's often affected by reflected light that puts a glow into the shadow. Make this glow by adding more Raw Sienna and some white into the shadow color. *IMPORTANT:* Make sure this value is darker than the sunlit side of the house. Get this reflected light value from your shadow mixture. Don't make up a new puddle to paint this value. This is the way to keep this value from getting too light.

Now, let's make the light side of the house even sunnier: take a lot of white and put the slightest, barest breath of Alizarin Crimson into it. Load a brush with this mixture and strike it over the sunlit side. The juxtaposition of the very light yellow of the first mixture with the very light violet you just put on gives the paint a chance to look vibrant.

If you like, put this last application on with a palette (or painting) knife. It's a good way to show the siding of the house, such as boards or shingles.

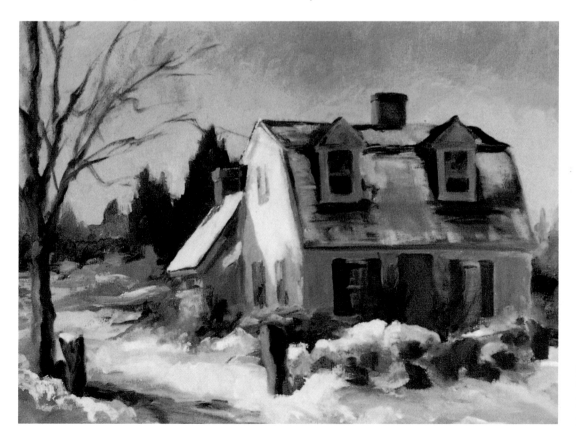

Rockport Cottage,
16 x 20",
Laura Elkins Stover
Private collection.

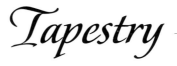

Tapestry

Painting a tapestry can by both exciting and frustrating, but — either way — well worth the experience. What follows is the procedure I have successfully used to create the effect of a woven fabric with a pictorial design worked in.

The first step is to prepare the canvas with a coat of acrylic paint which has been applied in a rough manner to imitate the feel of fabric. Do not apply this thickly, only roughly and with the very slightest tiny bumps and dents. (You can use oil colors for this stage, but you would have to wait much, much longer for it to dry thoroughly before being able to do the overpainting that the next step requires.)

When this is completely dry, paint the design you wish your tapestry to depict. Paint it in great detail, using oil paints from here on in. This second step needs to dry for a considerable amount of time. It has to be absolutely dry in order to complete the next stage in the procedure.

Once you are assured that your painting has dried completely, mix Raw Sienna with just a tiny bit of Yellow Ochre, being scrupulously careful not to use any medium or turpentine in this mixture. Load a large brush with the mixture, wipe gingerly with a cloth, and then drag the paint that remains on the brush lightly over your painting. Stroke your brush softly in, first, a vertical direction and then in a horizontal one, being careful to only let the "bumps" pick up a little of this mixture. This so-called "dry-brush" technique is what makes your design stay visible, with the dragging of the Raw Sienna and Yellow Ochre mixture over the whole, creating the illusion of fabric.

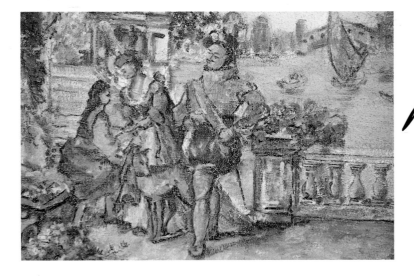

**Portrait of a Tapestry
(Details), 15 x 30",
oil on canvas,
Laura Elkins Stover,
*Private collection.***

Helpful Hint: If, for some awful reason, you make a mistake and put the paint on too heavily, the only thing to do is wash it off with turpentine, wait for it to dry and try again. Frustrating as this may be, it makes for a great learning experience. When it works, as I'm sure it will, it's such a grand and satisfying accomplishment. Good Luck.

Bas-Relief

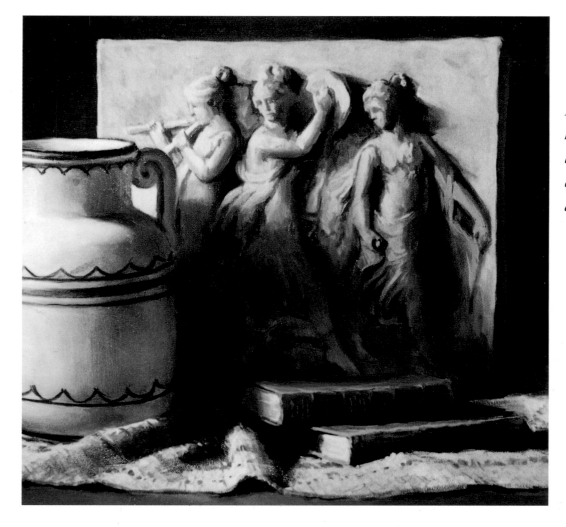

Painting a bas-relief is largely a matter of using cast shadows.

A bas-relief (also known as low relief) is a type of sculpture in which there's very little projection from the background. A bas-relief, injected into a composition, can help make an interesting subject in a painting. Painting this kind of sculpture is largely a matter of using cast shadows, just as you would do with a *trompe l'oeil* (pronounced trump loy) which is a still life whose objects all project from a flat surface.

1. Sketch the figures in with Burnt Sienna.

2. Into a light gray mixture of Ivory Black and white, add a little Yellow Ochre to paint the general tone of the background.

3. Using a mixture of Ivory Black, white and Burnt Sienna, paint the shadows on the figures.

4. In the deeper shadows on the figures, add a little Alizarin Crimson to the previous step's mixture.

5. Paint the light sides of the figures with a lighter gray mixture made of Ivory Black, white and Yellow Ochre in a tone that's lighter than the one used for the background.

6. Use a mixture of Ivory Black, white and a little Cadmium Orange for the reflections that are seen in the edges of the shadows on the figures.

7. Make the shadows on the background by mixing Burnt Umber into the general shadow color of Ivory Black and white, including a bit of Thalo Blue in the deep shadows.

Helpful Hint: The shadows of the figures on the background will make the figures protrude and have more substance, therefore, they have to be a great deal darker than the shadows on the figures themselves.

Copper Tray

What a fascinating texture to paint! And so colorful!

Here's a new approach that might help you get the correct tone values that are so important to painting copper.

1. Mix Cadmium Red Light and a little Cadmium Yellow Light into quite a large puddle of white. Load the brush with this very light pink mixture and paint in the areas that you see are the highlights.

2. Add Cadmium Orange and a little more of Cadmium Red Light into this mixture and paint around the highlights, cutting them down as you do. The stroking action can be such that it describes the tray's form .

3. Take Burnt Sienna and mix it into the mixture of *Step 2,* and mass in the remaining area of the tray.

4. Add a little Thalo Blue into the Burnt Sienna mixture and paint in any shadowed or darkened areas.

PLEASE NOTE: Instead of starting with a general tone — normally the procedure I prefer — this one starts with the lightest value and ends with the darkest value. I feel that this is the easiest way to give copper a shine because the highlight color has been applied to bare canvas instead of over a wet body tone, thus making it cleaner and fresher.

The highlight on copper is an exception to the rule of highlight color being complementary to the color it is on. The same principle applies to brass.

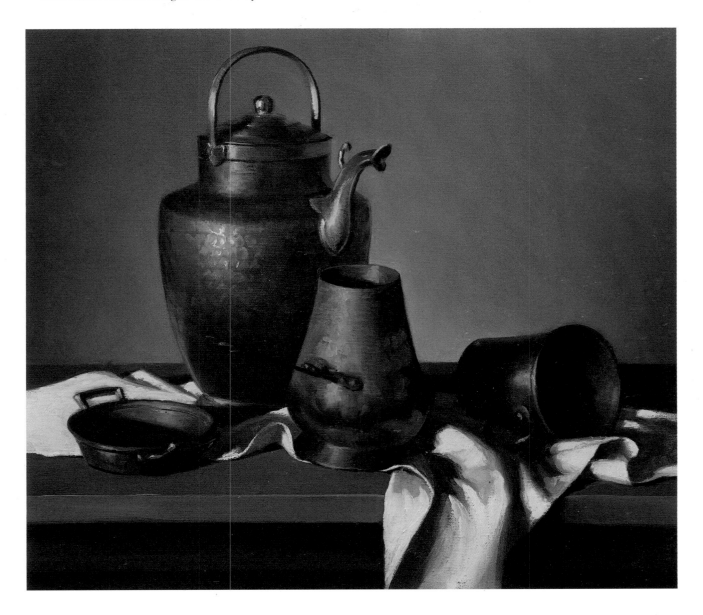

Brown Eggshells

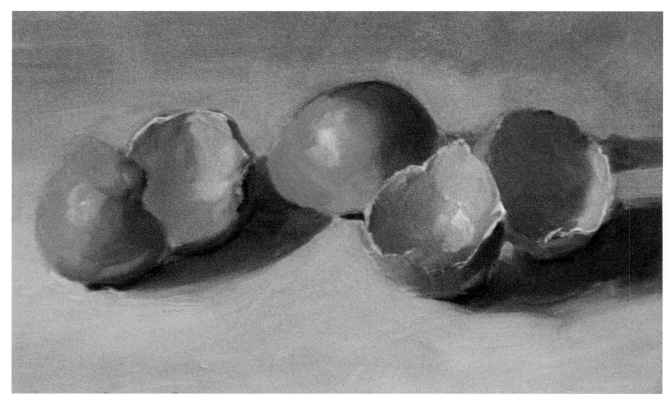

Eggshells, 3 x 6", oil on canvas, Laura Elkins Stover, *Private collection.*

Brown eggs, so typical of New England, are, strangely enough, harder to paint than white eggs. Their particular brownness varies, and their shells are less fragile. Moreover, the texture of brown egg shells has a doeskin look rather than the shell-like texture that we associate with white eggs. The shells themselves, cracked and painted alone, present an interesting and attractive addition to a painting, and are, indeed, an adventure in paint.

1. Mass in the brown part of the egg in a warm gray made with Ivory Black, white and Burnt Sienna.

2. Mass in the inside of the eggshell with a pinkish warm gray made with white, Ivory Black and a touch of Cadmium Red Light.

3. Where you see the outside of the egg in shadow, add a little Cobalt Blue to the mass tone, and in the light add more white and a little Cadmium Red Light.

4. In the shadowed area of the inside of the egg add a little more Ivory Black and the tiniest bit of Thalo Green to the mass tone; in the light area add more white and a bit of Yellow Ochre to the mass tone.

5. The highlight in the inside part of the egg is made by mixing white with a hint of Thalo Green.

6. The edge of the eggshells are part of the "adventure," and are painted with a mixture of white and just a bit of Yellow Ochre. Use a very sharp-edged flat sable brush and scoop a little of this to carefully indicate the edges of the eggshell as they protrude forward into the light. Add a little Ivory Black to this mixture where the edges are away from the light.

7. Into the shadowed side of the eggs add a warm gray reflected light by mixing Burnt Sienna, Cadmium Orange and a little white into the shadow mixture.

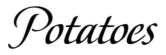

Potatoes

While I have rarely used potatoes as subjects in my still lifes, I can see how they can be utilized in a composition with a cooking theme. Since the color of most potatoes is that dull brown which is uninteresting, I have chosen red potatoes and sweet potatoes to feature here. At least, there is *some* color in those two varieties.

Red Potatoes

1. Mass in the potato with a mixture of Alizarin Crimson, a small amount of Burnt Umber and gray (Ivory Black and white).
2. Into this mixture, add more Alizarin Crimson, a little Cadmium Red Light and a breath of Sap Green to paint the shadowed side of the potato.
3. Where the light strikes, mix Grumbacher Red, a little Cadmium Red Light and white.
4. The highlight is white with the barest touch of Viridian.

Sweet Potatoes

1. Mass the whole potato in with a mixture of Burnt Sienna, Burnt Umber and gray (Ivory Black and white) and just a touch of Cadmium Red Light. Into this mixture, add more Burnt Umber and a little Thalo Blue to paint the shadowed side of the potato.
2. Where the light strikes, mix Cadmium Orange, a tiny bit of Cadmium Red Light and a little white.
3. The highlight, not too prominent on subjects like these, is made with white and very little Thalo Blue.

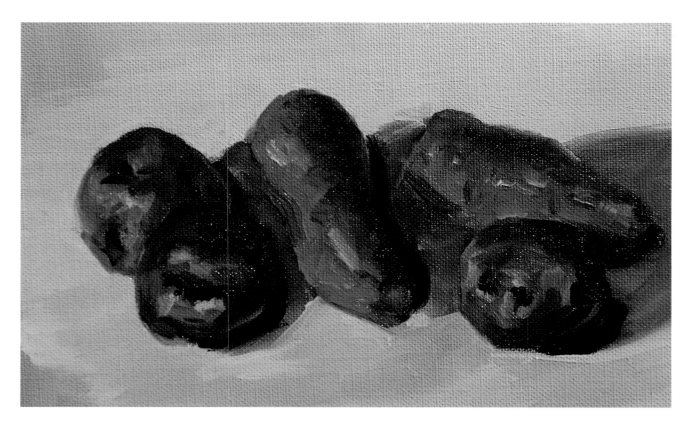

Helpful Hint: The eyes of the red potato are quite red and can be painted with Grumbacher Red. The slight haze you see on the light side of the potato can be applied with a grayish mixture made by mixing white, a little Grumbacher Red and a little Viridian.

Helpful Hint: There is a dullness to the surface of the sweet potato, and this can be indicated by mixing a gray of Ivory Black and white into Cadmium Orange. This should be quite light, but applied carefully so that it just skims over the surface in light.

Corn

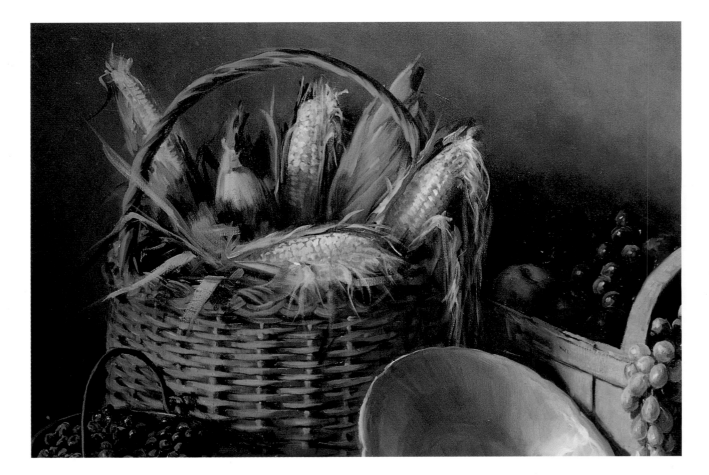

Here's subject matter that for most of the country provides some inspiration every summer. Corn is fascinating to add into any composition along with baskets, tomatoes, cucumbers and other vegetables that are so symbolic of summertime.

Mass in the entire ear of corn with a mixture that's much darker than you see when looking at the corn. Make this mixture with Raw Sienna, Yellow Ochre, a touch of Cadmium Yellow Medium and just a little gray made of Ivory Black and white.

Into this mixture add Alizarin Crimson and a touch of Ivory Black for the shadowed side of the corn.

Where the light strikes, mix Cadmium Yellow Light and white, then adding Cadmium Yellow Medium as it turns into shadow.

When painting the kernels, you don't, of course, want to paint each individual one, but you do want to indicate with lights and darks their existence on the cob. Therefore, paint the shadowed side with a mixture of Raw Sienna and Cadmium Yellow Medium. Paint the light side with highlights that are made with white and a very little bit of Alizarin Crimson.

Helpful Hint: As for the procedure in painting the rows of kernels, paint them unevenly in bumps and then plop on the highlights, using a palette knife to complete the illusion.

Indian Corn

Indian corn is colorful and decorative. I find it useful and attractive for fall arrangements. Although it's not for human consumption, the birds seem to have a very good time feasting on the ears that I usually hang on my front door at the start of each Autumn season.

Indian corn comes in a variety of fall colors: dark red, yellow, shades of Burnt Sienna and Yellow Ochre.

1. Mass in the ears with a rich red made of Alizarin Crimson, Burnt Umber and a little Burnt Sienna.

2. Into this mixture, add more Burnt Umber and a little Thalo Blue to paint the shadowed side of the ear.

3. The kernels on the side where the light strikes are painted with Grumbacher Red, Cadmium Red Light and just a bit of Alizarin Crimson. Some of these kernels may appear orange and where you see this, add Cadmium Orange. Put these on roughly to indicate that it is dried corn, and highlight a few of the kernels with white and just a touch of Viridian.

4. The dried husks are massed in with Raw Sienna, gray (Ivory Black and white) and just a bit of Burnt Sienna.

5. Mix white, Yellow Ochre and just a touch of Cadmium Orange to paint the husks where the light strikes, using a palette knife to strike the paint on sharply.

6. The husks in shadow are painted with Raw Sienna, Yellow Ochre and just a little Cadmium Orange. Darker darks may be added with Burnt Umber.

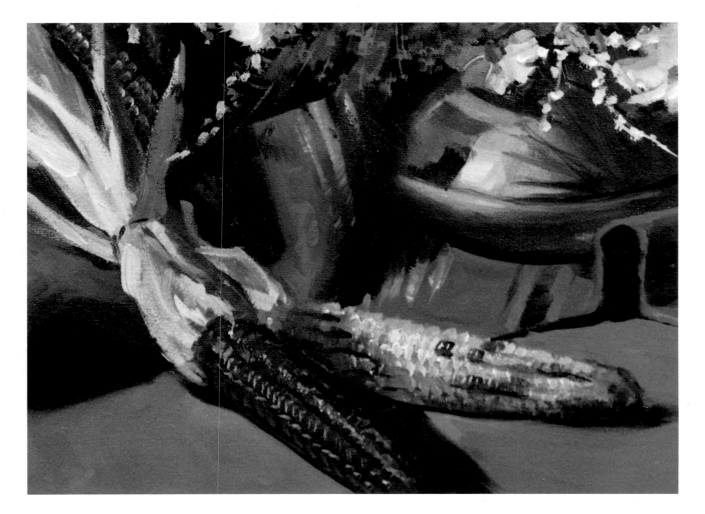

Carrots

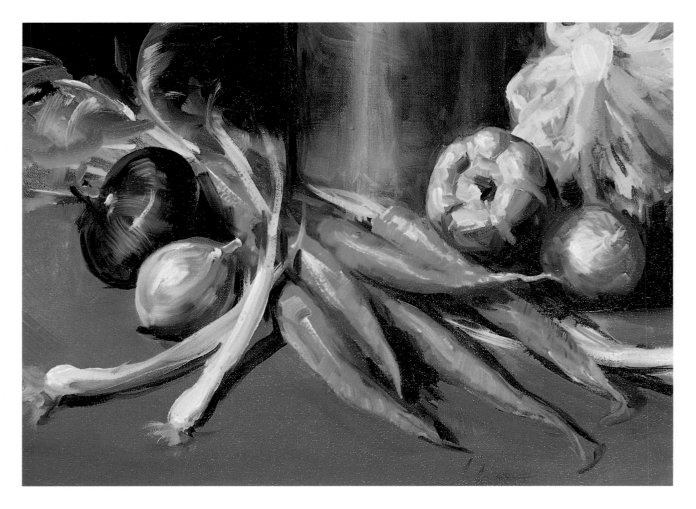

When painting carrots, it's best to leave the tops on; they will look more natural and will be easier to describe in paint. Furthermore, always position them in a way to make them an asset to your painting.

1. With Raw Sienna, a little Cadmium Red Light and white, mass in the carrots.

2. Add a little Burnt Sienna and a touch of Thalo Blue to the mass tone to paint the shadowed side of the carrots.

3. Mix Cadmium Orange, white and Cadmium Yellow Light for the light side of the carrot. Add a touch of Thalo Yellow Green at the big end of the carrot.

4. The highlight should be white with a hint of Thalo Blue. Be aware of the ridges that ring around the carrot, making sure to paint your highlight in a way that will not "smooth out" this important characteristic.

5. The greenery of the carrot is painted with a mixture of white, Raw Sienna and Thalo Yellow Green on the light side and Sap Green mixed with a little Grumbacher Red for the darker areas.

Garlic

In my kitchen, garlic is as much a staple food as milk and bread are. As a cook, garlic gives me a marvelous ingredient for almost all of my recipes. As a painter, garlic has provided me with a fascinating addition, along with cooking pots and other vegetables, to a number of still life compositions.

1. Mass in the general shape of the garlic in a darker version of the color you see. This can generally be made by mixing Ivory Black, white, Yellow Ochre and the tiniest bit of Alizarin Crimson.

2. Into the shadowed side, add to this mixture Raw Sienna and a little more Alizarin Crimson. Paint this shadowed area in such a manner as to describe the individual cloves of garlic on the dark side.

3. On the light side, sculpt the individual garlic cloves with white, a bit of Ivory Black and a little Yellow Ochre, adding Alizarin Crimson as the clove turns into shadow.

4. With white and a touch of Yellow Ochre, define the very lightest parts of the garlic, being careful not to overdo this and destroy the delicate shapes of the cloves.

5. If you see a highlight, it will be made by mixing a hint of Alizarin Crimson into a puddle of white, blending it gently into the already painted light parts.

6. The reflection in the shadowed side of the garlic cloves may be added with a grayed version of the mass tone.

7. Sometimes showing the root end of the garlic may add interest. These roots should be painted with Raw Sienna in the lighter part and a bit of Burnt Sienna and Cobalt Blue added to the darker parts. Where the light strikes more strongly, add Yellow Ochre and a bit of white to these delicate roots.

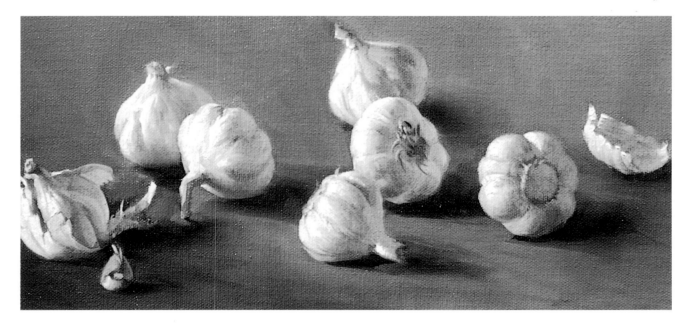

As a painter, garlic has provided me with a fascinating addition to a number of still life compositions.

Yellow Onions

The marvelous shine of onions is described in paint by a highlight. If you can't get this highlight, you'll never make your onion look like an onion. Herewith, some colors and procedures to help you:

1. Draw the shape of the onion. Show the view that's most descriptive: the base (where the roots were) or the top (where the blossoms were), but not coming at you like bull's-eyes.

2. Move a quarter of a teaspoon of white to a clean place on your palette. Add into it a very little Alizarin Crimson or Thalo Red Rose. Keep this puddle fresh. Don't stir into it too much. Scoop this very, very light violet onto your brush and gob it onto the drawing of the onion where you see the highlight. It should be bigger than the highlight actually is. This is shown in *Step 1*.

3. Wipe your brush with a rag. Take a little white and add Cadmium Yellow Light and a touch of Burnt Sienna. Paint this color around the highlight, cutting the highlight down in size.

4. Mass in the rest of the onion with Burnt Sienna, Cadmium Orange, and Cadmium Yellow Light (mixed in that order). Use white to lighten this mass tone just enough so it's darker than the mixture in *Step 3*.

5. Into this mixture add some Alizarin Crimson and a touch of Ivory Black for the shadows. Important: All the applications in *Steps 2, 3, & 4* should be opposite to the lines of the onion skin.

6. Now the fun starts, if you have enough paint on the canvas and have a nice soft brush (#14 red sable Bright or a large red sable round): Stroke into the paint in the direction of the lines in the onion's skin, even right through the highlight. You'll see the paint move together and the effect of the onion's skin will appear. This may not happen the first time. An unskilled, heavy hand can push these mixtures right into the oblivion of one value. Your first experience will most likely tell you that you didn't have enough paint loaded on the highlight area, and that you may have also skimped on the other mixtures. If the stroking can't dig into a layer of paint, you're apt to press too hard as you stroke, which will mush the colors too much together. This is shown in *Step 2*.

7. Any peculiarity of the onion, such as red, yellow, pink, or green colorations, should be painted in before the stroking action.

8. Finally, the highlight will have to be applied again, more carefully than initially. Use the same mixture as used in *Step 2*. This is shown in *Step 3*.

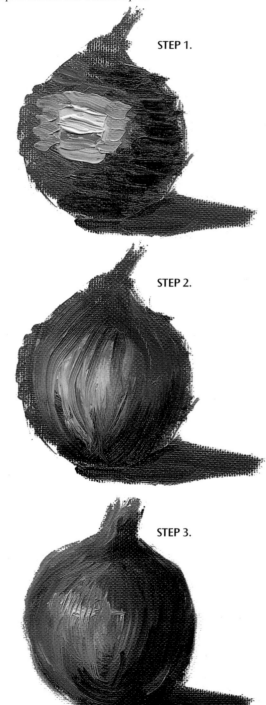

STEP 1.

STEP 2.

STEP 3.

Red Onions

Here's a colorful subject to paint! Paint them by themselves. Arrange them interestingly on a white cloth. String them together and hang them from a hook or nail. Red onions also present a colorful accent in an arrangement of vegetables. (For procedure, refer to Yellow Onions.)

Now for the colors to paint red onions:

1. Mix a little bit of Thalo Green into a lot of white and paint this where you see the onion shine (the highlight).

2. Surround this highlight area with white, Cadmium Orange, and Thalo Red Rose.

3. Take pure Thalo Red Rose and paint it in the area around the mixture of *Step 2.*

4. The basic tone is Alizarin Crimson and Burnt Sienna mixed.

5. Put a little bit of Thalo Green into Alizarin Crimson and paint in the shadow that's only visible where the onion's shape falls away from the source of light.

6. The intriguing reflection of the onion's surroundings is tempting to paint. It's best to do this last, and only after the painting of the onion has somewhat dried. This reflection color is Ivory Black and white mixed plus Alizarin Crimson and Thalo Green — very gray. Another way: Mass the entire onion in the mass tone mixture first, then add the color to it to show the highlight.

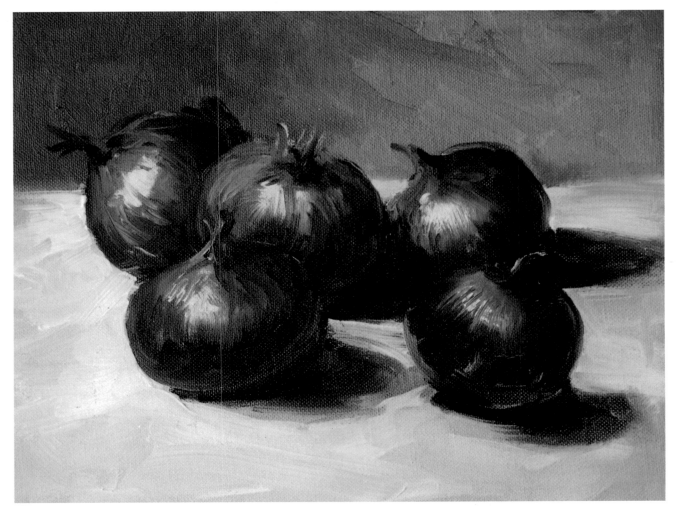

Red Onions, 11 x 15", oil on canvas, Laura Elkins Stover, *Private collection.*

Lettuce and Cabbage

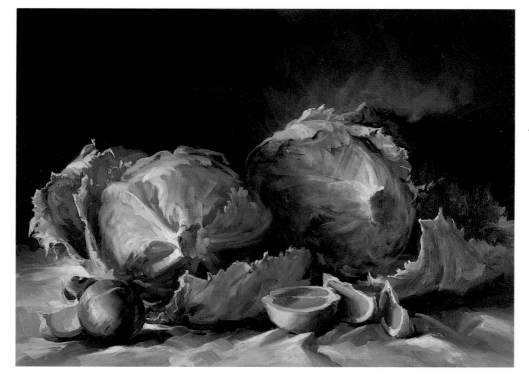

When painting lettuce and cabbage you're working with a round shape that's best recorded with a light side and a dark side.

Strange subject matter? Not really when you consider that as long as the subject intrigues the artist everything in sight is a possible picture. Just consider what Chardin has done with dead fish, or what Monet did with asparagus.

No matter what you paint, keep in mind that a successful rendition is the result of *a very keen observation* of the subject matter. Also, give yourself an added edge by putting your subject in advantageous lighting and in a position where you'll be looking at the view that's most descriptive of the subject.

Now for procedure and color: The colors used for lettuce and cabbage are very much the same; your observations of these objects will determine whether you're painting a lettuce or a cabbage. Either one can be included in an arrangement with tomatoes, onions, carrots, cucumbers and mushrooms, along with a bowl or a large wine bottle. This arrangement indicates the making of a salad; it should give you some sort of idea of the ways to include these leafy vegetables in a composition.

1. Remember, when painting lettuce and cabbage you're working with a round shape that's best recorded with a light side and a dark side. Don't get so involved with the leaves or the veins of the leaves that you overlook the fact that you're painting a bulky, three-dimensional object that must look three-dimensional on your flat, two-dimensional canvas. Guarantee this dimensional look by massing in the entire lettuce or cabbage area in the darkest color you see on the light side. Most likely, this will be a mixture of Thalo Yellow Green, Burnt Umber, Thalo Green, Ivory Black, and a little white.

2. Put more black, Thalo Yellow Green and a little Alizarin Crimson into the previous mixture and paint in wherever you see the round form of the head fall away from the light. This mixture should have a muted violet look.

3. You now have the silhouette of the form and a feeling of dimension onto which you can add lights and darks to further develop the mass as a lettuce or a cabbage. Do so by adding lights of Thalo Yellow Green into white for the veins and then make even lighter veins with white, a breath of Alizarin Crimson and a touch of Ivory Black, giving you a violet off-white.

4. Strike in some mixtures of brighter, lighter color, most likely white, Cadmium Yellow Light, and a little Thalo Green. Darken some of the areas with Ivory Black, white, Thalo Green and Cadmium Orange.

Beets

When doing a painting of beets, it's important to arrange them in such a manner as to show off their shapes to advantage. Beets have little roots (I call them tails) that help describe their shape and character and, along with their bright green leaves with red veins and stems, they make a fascinating subject for a painting.

1. Mass in the shape of the beet with Alizarin Crimson and a touch of Thalo Blue, leaving the root to do later. With that same mixture, paint the stems being careful not to get them too thick.

2. Add more Thalo Blue to the mixture for the shadowed side of the beet.

3. With a mixture made of Alizarin Crimson, a little Thalo Red Rose and a touch of Grumbacher Red, paint the light side of the beet.

4. Add a little white to Thalo Red Rose to paint in the highlight area. This should not be a bright highlight but a blush of color.

5. With a mixture of light gray (Ivory Black, white and a bit of Viridian) drag over the light areas of the beet to produce the dull shine that's so characteristic of beets. This mixture may also be applied to the root after it has been defined with the beet mass tone.

6. Mass the leaves in with Sap Green and a little Alizarin Crimson.

7. Paint the lighter parts of the leaves with a mixture of Thalo Green, Sap Green and a touch of Viridian.

Helpful Hint: Paint the leaves in a ruffled manner. Remember to show the red veins that are so characteristic of beet greens. Use Alizarin Crimson and some Thalo Red Rose for this.

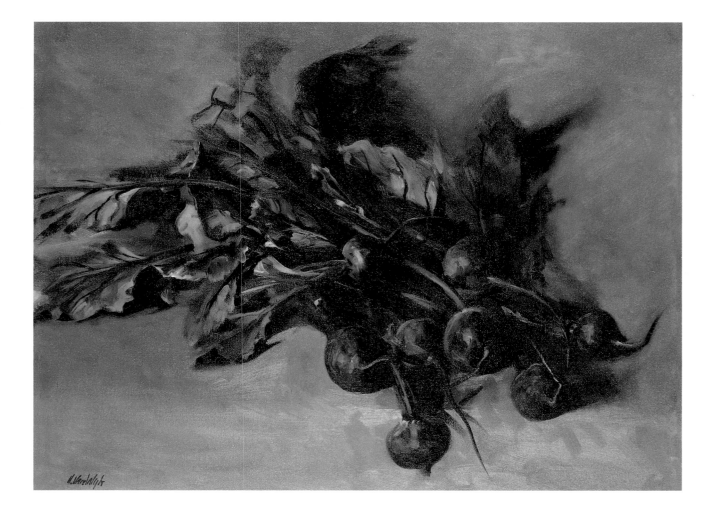

Pumpkins

Other than its bright orange color, an identifying characteristic of a pumpkin are the ridged sections of its shape, each having a light side and a dark side. Here are the mixtures:

1. Paint the entire pumpkin with a mixture of Burnt Sienna, a touch of Cadmium Red Light and a little gray of Ivory Black and white. Or Burnt Sienna, a touch of Cadmium Red Light and some Cobalt Blue.

2. Where the ridges meet the light, mix white with Cadmium Orange, a speck of Burnt Sienna, touch of Cadmium Red Light and Cadmium Yellow Medium. Work this carefully into the front part of the ridge toward the light and blend where it meets the shadow with Cadmium Orange and the barest amount of Cobalt Blue. As the ridges get closer to the shadowed side of the pumpkin, these separations of color will be less apparent, in most cases identified with the reflective tone.

3. In the lightest sections, use more Cadmium Yellow Medium than in the previous mixture and make a highlight by adding just a touch of Thalo Blue in a puddle of white. Brush this on carefully where you see the light strike, and work it in with Cadmium Yellow Medium until it appears as a blush.

4. The stems have their own ridges as well, so the initial painting of them would be done in a mixture of Sap Green, Raw Sienna and a little gray. The lighter ridges will be identified with a paint mixture of this basic mix and adding Thalo Yellow Green, a little more white and a bit of Yellow Ochre. Where the stem attaches to the pumpkin, there are dark shadows on the side away from the light. These can be made by adding a touch of Alizarin Crimson to Burnt Umber and a dark gray.

5. Reflections in the dark side of the pumpkin are made with Raw Sienna, a little Cadmium Orange into gray, a darker value by far than anything on the light side.

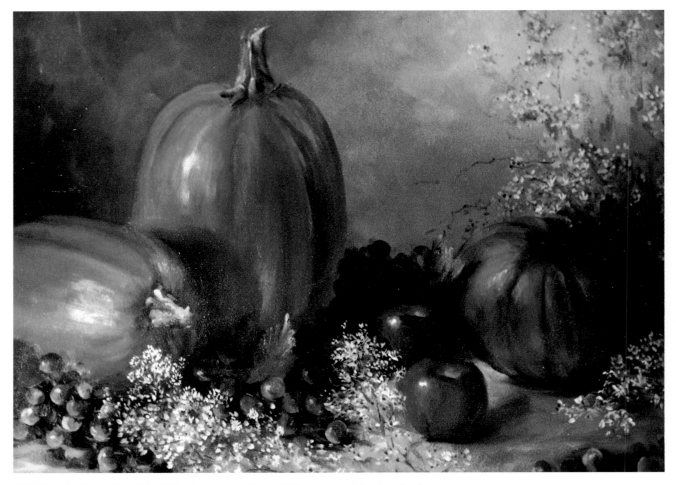

Still Life with Pumpkins, 16 x 20", oil on canvas, Laura Elkins Stover, *Private collection*.

Red and Purple Plums

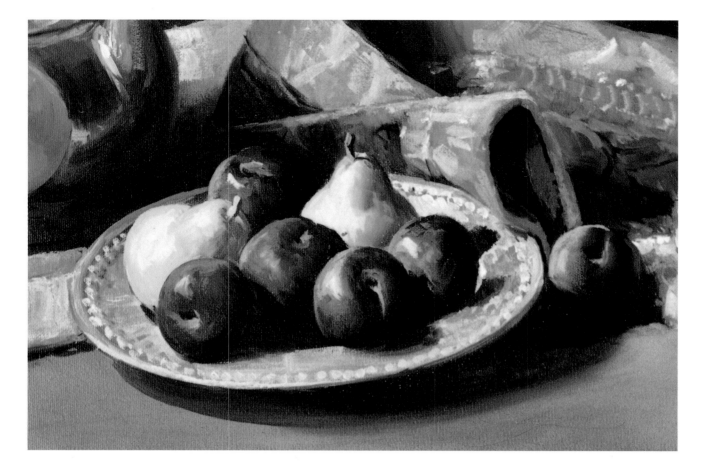

Plums, like peaches, have a distinctive shape. If arranged in a way that the light accentuates this shape, it can be a great help in describing them in paint. The haze on plums, more evident on the purple than on the red, is an identifying feature and should always be painted.

Purple Plums

1. Mass the plum in with a mixture of Alizarin Crimson, a little Thalo Blue and a tiny bit of white.

2. Where the light strikes the strongest thus creating a more reddish color, mix a little Grumbacher Red and Alizarin Crimson into a gray of Ivory Black and white. Fuse this carefully with the darker mixture so that the plum has just a hint of a rosy glow.

3. On the shadowed side of the plum, add a little Burnt Umber and more Thalo Blue to the mass-tone mixture.

4. To paint the haze, mix Ivory Black, white, and the barest hint of Thalo Blue and drag this color over the areas where you see it in light. Do this when the painting has been dried.

5. The reflection on the shadowed side of the plum is painted with a grayed mixture of the mass tone color.

6. Paint the highlight with white and a very small addition of Viridian.

Red Plums

1. Mass in the plum with a mixture of Alizarin Crimson, Grumbacher Red, a little Yellow Ochre into a gray of Ivory Black and white. Into the shadowed side, add a little Sap Green and more Alizarin Crimson.

2. On the light side, mix Yellow Ochre, Cadmium Red Light and a speck of Grumbacher Red.

3. The highlight is made by adding a small amount of Thalo Yellow Green to white; the reflection is made by mixing Ivory Black, white and a little Grumbacher Red, added to the edge of the shadowed side.

4. The haze is added by mixing a gray of Ivory Black and white.

Lemons

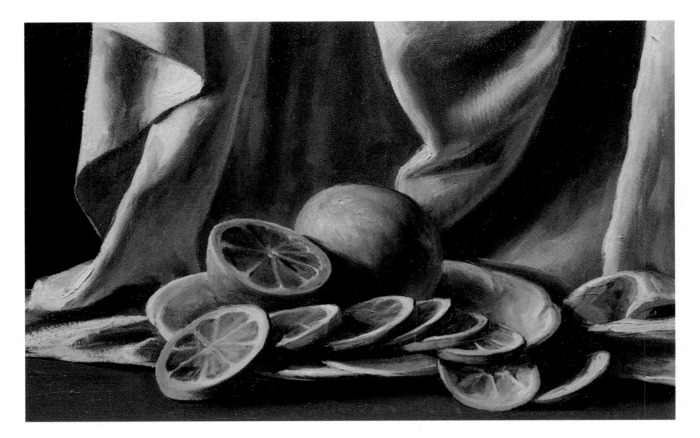

Probably the most versatile fruit for the still life painter, a lemon can be used with tea cups, teapots, and flowers because a lemon is associated with tea. Also, because lemons are used for cooking, salads, etc., they may be included with many vegetables. Sometimes, the lemon provides just the spark of color you need in an arrangement. A lemon can also be used by itself to make an intriguing picture. I recall vividly a beautiful Dutch still life showing a lemon's partially pared peel spiraling over a table's edge. *REMEMBER:* It's not what you paint that's important, it's how you paint it.

1. Place and see a good view of the lemon. Never have either the lemon's stem or knob end facing you head on.

2. Mass the lemon in with Cadmium Yellow Medium. If the lemon is more of the greenish-yellow type, add a touch of Thalo Yellow Green to the Cadmium Yellow Medium.

3. To paint the shadow, mix a puddle of Ivory Black and white and Alizarin Crimson (or any other violet) in a tone a few shades darker than the mass tone. Put this mixture into the mass tone mixture and use this color for the shadow. The value of the shadow depends on the lighting that you use. The stronger the light the darker the shadow. For darker shadows, add some Ultramarine Blue to your shadow mixture.

4. Mix Cadmium Yellow Medium, Cadmium Yellow Light and white and lighten the value of the mass tone where the lemon is more in line with the light. This is best piled on in dabs to give the appearance of the lemon's porous skin.

5. To make the lemon shine, add a highlight of white with a breath of Alizarin Crimson in it. Pat this on with little dabs.

6. For the reflected lights in the shadow, use a little Raw Sienna or Cadmium Yellow Medium. If the lemon's on a white cloth, the reflected light can be quite light. Use some light gray with Cadmium Yellow Light.

Blueberries

An important consideration when painting blueberries is to try not to make them too blue or too purple. A good way to avoid this is to make your mixtures with either gray or the complement of the color used. Blueberries — especially when seen in the sunshine — have a wonderful grayish haze which is an important feature to record if you are to make them look realistic.

1. Blueberries are seen in a bowl or growing in a cluster on a bush. In a bowl, mass in the general shape of the berries with a mixture of gray (black and white), Burnt Umber and a touch of Thalo Blue. As seen on the bush, try to keep the bunch very loose and not as closely clustered as with grapes.

2. Add to this mixture (either one) a little more Thalo Blue, a little Alizarin Crimson and a touch of Burnt Umber to paint the shadows as you see them on the berries.

3. Not every blueberry will be in direct light so not every one will appear round; some will overlap others, creating variety and indicating proper perspective and a feeling of depth.

4. Mix a light gray blue-violet — Ivory Black and white, Alizarin Crimson with a touch of Thalo Blue — and work this lighter blue-violet tone wherever you see the light strike a berry.

5. To paint the haze on the blueberries, mix a tiny bit of Cerulean Blue into a light gray (made of Ivory Black and white) and drag this color over the berries, adding more white wherever you see a highlight. Be careful to show a light side and a dark side of each berry to show roundness. A tiny reflection can be added on the dark side by mixing a bit of Alizarin Crimson and a touch of Thalo Blue and white. This will give it a slight translucent quality.

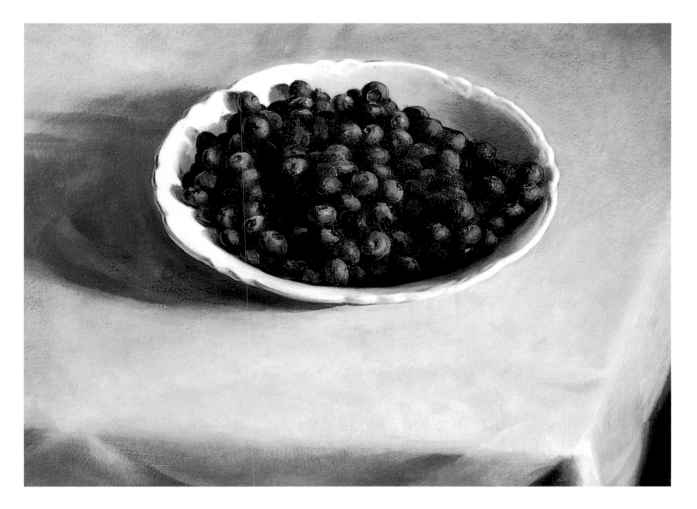

Strawberries

The strawberry is a delicious looking fruit, presenting the painter with the fun of describing its many shades of red and its luscious and juicy quality — all with paint. Painted alone, or in a group with other fruit or still life arrangements, strawberries add a beautiful touch of color and interest to many compositions.

1. Mass the strawberries in with a mixture of Alizarin Crimson and Grumbacher Red, keeping this application rather thin. Lighter red will be added later, and a too-thick application will make this application difficult to do.

2. Into the shadow side add a bit of Thalo Green to the mass tone, and apply it carefully to show the shape of the strawberry.

3. The light side of the strawberry is painted with a mixture of Cadmium Red Light and just a touch of Cadmium Yellow Light and white, blending this into the shadow side with Grumbacher Red..

4. The tiny seeds you see on the strawberry are an important identifying characteristic, but should be done discriminately. Adding too many will look very strange, and won't create the effect you're looking for. On the dark side of the strawberry use Yellow Ochre applied with a tiny brush, adding Alizarin Crimson on the shadow side of the seed. Remember, do not add too many. On the light side, the seed may be done with Cadmium Yellow Light, and shadowed with Grumbacher Red. The seed is dimpled into the strawberry, so with a tiny bit of Thalo Green into a lot of white, paint the light side with little strokes to indicate these dimpled areas, thus creating the look of seeds without actually painting each one. This is often easier and more effectively done by dragging this mixture carefully over the dried area in question.

5. The highlight on the strawberry is done with white and the tiniest bit of Thalo Green, and accentuated with a lighter version of the light side mixture to make it shine.

6. Into the dark side of the strawberry, add a reflection with gray (black and white) and a bit of Thalo Green.

Helpful Hint: You'll find that you'll be going back and forth applying these basic color mixtures to get the look of the strawberry as you see it, and that the strokes you use will be important. The strawberry doesn't appear to be smooth, therefore, the strokes should indicate this, and they should be short and descriptive.

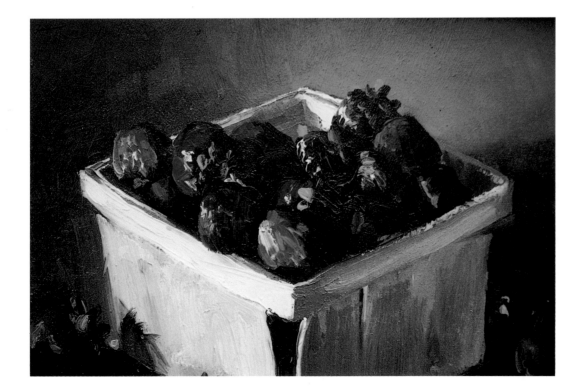

Bananas

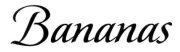

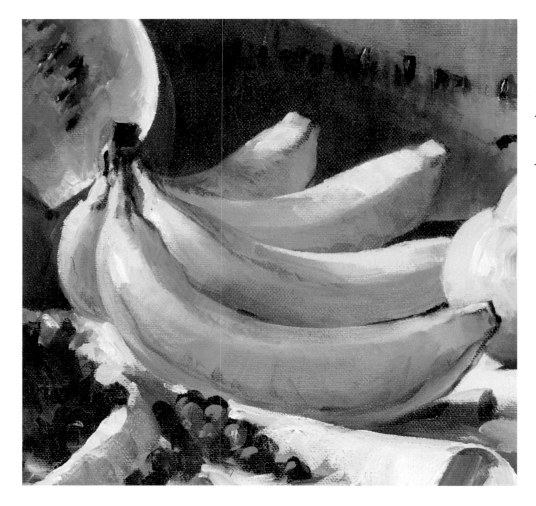

Don't let the peculiar shapes of bananas lead your eye out of the picture.

For many years I had discouraged all students' attempts to include bananas in a fruit arrangement because they posed such a problem in composition. In a fruit arrangement, a banana can stick out like a sore thumb if it's not painted or positioned right. When arranging bananas with other fruits, don't let their peculiar shapes lead your eye out of the picture. And if you've got them lying on a table, break the line by placing a round fruit in front of the banana. Here's how to paint bananas after you've carefully included this subject in a composition.

1. The colors for bananas: Where the light strikes the bananas, mass in with Cadmium Yellow Light toned with Manganese Violet. Use Thalo Yellow Green with Manganese Violet for the less ripe bananas.

2. For the shadowed planes and cast shadows on the bananas: Mix Manganese Violet and Yellow Ochre.

3. Paint the light and dark masses with strokes that travel in the direction of the length of the banana.

4. The lighter lights should be applied in Cadmium Yellow Light, Yellow Ochre and white. Use quite a bit of paint and stroke in a direction that's opposite from the way you originally painted it.

5. Where you see the banana quite light, use Cadmium Yellow Light mixed into a light gray.

6. Put some color back into the shadows by using Raw Sienna with a touch of Cadmium Yellow Medium.

7. Put in the darker shadows with Manganese Violet and Burnt Umber.

8. Now for any bruises you may see on the banana.
   Caution: Don't make them too dark! Mix a little Burnt Umber or Burnt Sienna — depending on how brown or orange the blemish is — and first mix this color into the yellow banana color on your palette before you apply it to your painting. This adjusts the blemish color to the tone that it's going to be on.

Siamese Cat

I never liked the Siamese cat that my first husband and I owned. However, it didn't stop me from painting it.

1. Mass in the cat's entire body with a mixture of Burnt Sienna, Burnt Umber, Raw Sienna and gray (Ivory Black and white).

2. Add more Burnt Umber, a little Alizarin Crimson and Ivory Black to this mixture to paint the dark places of the cat: the legs and paws, head and ears.

3. With Raw Sienna, Yellow Ochre and a little white, paint the lighter portions of the cat's body with short, hair-like strokes, letting some of the mass tone show through. Where the light strikes strongest, add more white and just a touch of Cadmium Orange to this mixture. Where this color turns into shadow, add more Burnt Sienna, a little Burnt Umber and a little Thalo Blue to this mixture and then paint it on carefully with strokes that indicate soft fur.

4. Into the shadowed sides of the darker areas, add more Burnt Umber, Ivory Black and a little Thalo Blue and blend this into the darkest-toned places, blending to meet the lighter portions with strokes of Burnt Sienna and a little Thalo Blue.

5. Make a mixture of Ivory Black, white and Thalo Blue to pick out the lighter portions of the dark areas: around the eyes and on top of the nose area. This dark blue-gray may also be used to paint the pads on the cat's paws and for the whiskers that appear as light against the dark side.

6. The eyes are painted with a grayed mixture of Thalo Green with just a bit of Yellow Ochre added; the pupils with Ivory Black. Make the highlight with white and just a touch of Alizarin Crimson to gray it.

Helpful Hint: A very soft Hake (pronounced Hockey) brush will help you get the fur-like strokes that appear on the cat's body. Use short strokes and carefully blend one color into the other.

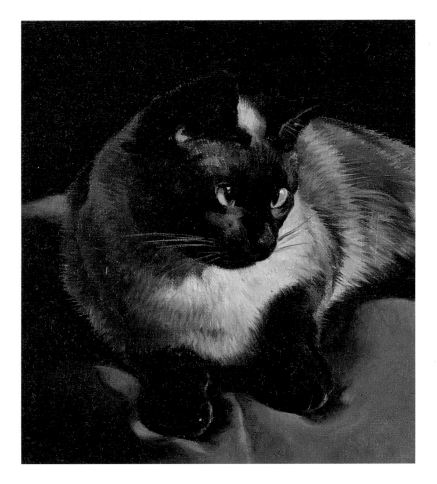

Collie

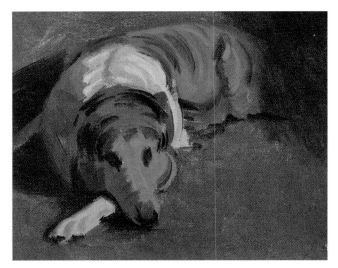

FIGURE 1.

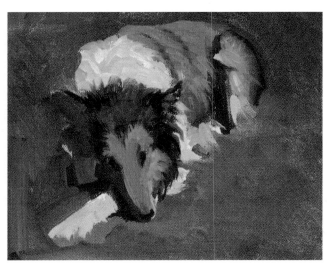

FIGURE 2.

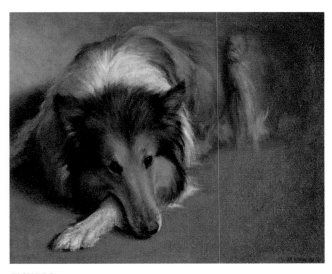

FIGURE 3.

To paint a number of animals, you can use a basic mixture that would apply to most of them. The color mixtures, of course, can be helpful, but it's more important to know how to apply these mixtures and the way to record the texture of hair.

THE BASIC MIXTURE: Burnt Sienna, Cadmium Orange into white and a little Cerulean Blue to tone the color down.

THE SHADOWS: Add Burnt Sienna, Burnt Umber and a little Ultramarine Blue and Alizarin Crimson to the basic mixture.

THE SHINE ON THE HAIR: White and a touch of black with Alizarin Crimson.

Now for the all-important paint application:

1. This is a good example of how I applied my paint in strokes that are opposite to the way the hair grows. I also cut my background into the outer shape of the dog, saving the final effect of the texture for the final stroking. Never use the final effect for the massing-in stage, a mistake that's prevalent among most beginners.

2. Here we see how a careful progression of stroking was used to overlap the hair, showing that the ears are in front of the white neck hair and how overlapping out into the background with hair strokes makes the dog look as though she were lying on the green rug. Always proceed with a careful awareness of what's in front of what and then proceed accordingly.

3. In this final step, I enlarged the eyes and nose into the correct shape and added lighter and darker accents on the hair.

My Collie, 20 x 24", *Private collection.*
The finished painting.

West Highland Terriers

This subject is best done from photographs. Make sure you work from photos of the dog that have good contrasts of light and dark, ruling out flashbulb snapshots.

1. Since Westies are white, and are most often a yellowish white, use yellow's complement, violet (Alizarin Crimson, Ivory Black and white), and paint in all the shadows. Make these shadows a little bigger than they really are. Paint in the darks that you see when you squint at the photo rather than what you see with your eyes wide open. *Squint! Squint! Squint!*

2. Now, put in the background. (The only area left will be the white canvas that represents the light where it strikes the dog.) For the first application in the background, use a grayed-down version of the color you want. If you use too strong a color at this time it might bleed into the light tone you'll be using to record the Westie's fluffy hair. So — instead of a white Westie, you'll end up getting one that's a lighter version of your background color. (Who ever heard of a Pink Westie?)

   However, by first using a grayed version of your background color, you'll stand less chance of contaminating the dog's color wherever it meets the background. After the dog's done, you can always redo the background with a brighter color.

3. Fill in wherever the white dog is light with a mixture of Burnt Umber, Raw Sienna, and a lot of white (adding a little bit of Cobalt Blue won't hurt this mixture). Fill in and sculpt this color into the shadows and against the background, making this light shape correctly fitted to both the background and the shadow. Naturally, where the hair touches the background the tone should meet the background in a fuzzy way. You can often do this better with your finger than with a brush.

4. Add more white to this mixture and accentuate the light shape wherever you see it lighter.

5. Into the violet shadows add a mixture of Ivory Black and white and Raw Sienna, and try to impart some feeling of texture into the shadow side.

6. With a dark gray made of Burnt Umber, a little white, and touch of Ultramarine Blue, paint in the darks for the nose and the eyes. Accentuate with shadows of Alizarin Crimson and Thalo Blue.

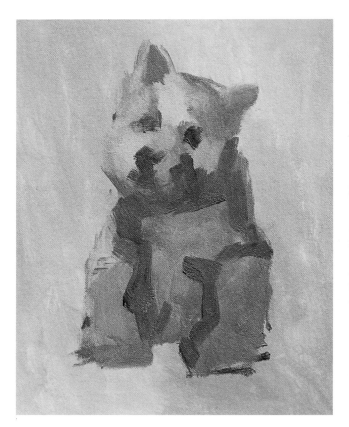

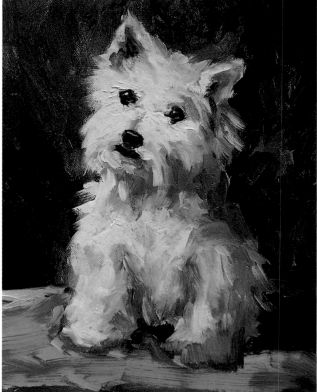

Irish Setters

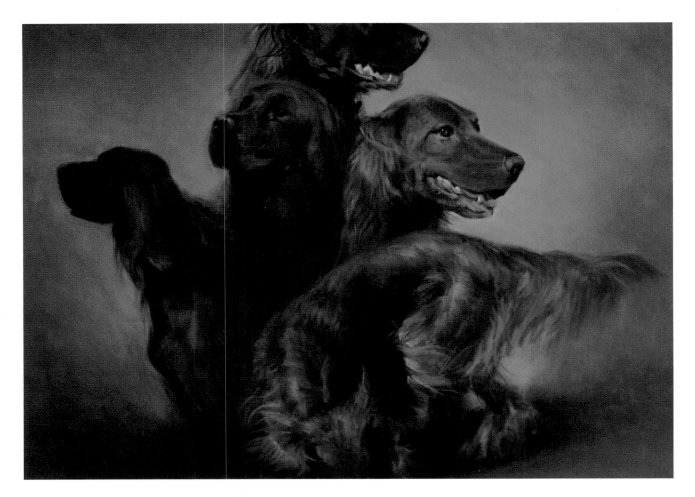

An Irish setter is a large and friendly animal, loved by many as a family pet and loyal companion. He has long and silky hair, and a beautiful square-type head that's characterized by expressive, kindly eyes. Setters are rusty in color which says "Burnt Sienna." The following are the mixtures for painting this marvelous dog.

1. Mass the general shape of the setter with a mixture of Burnt Sienna, a little Yellow Ochre and just a bit of white.

2. Into this mixture, add Burnt Sienna, Burnt Umber and a touch of Cobalt Blue for the shadowed parts you see.

3. The light parts are painted with a mixture of Burnt Sienna, a bit of Yellow Ochre and white, painting with strokes that indicate the fur as it lies over the body and not completely covering the initial mass tone. Squint as you do this, trying to have the strokes show the shape of the animal as the light hits it.

4. When painting the head use small strokes in the direction the hair falls around the eyes and as it grows near and over the ears. The eyes are painted, taking careful note of their shape, much as the human eye is painted: a highlight and a spot of color indicating the light traveling through the eye from the highlight.

5. Where the shine on the fur occurs, mix a little Cobalt Blue into white and paint it on the fur in a crosswise stroke, then "comb" it with a dry brush to show the shine. This should be done most carefully and not in too large an area because it will detract from rather then enhance the appearance of the fur.

Helpful Hint: Even if you own an Irish setter and feel you know everything about the breed, do not attempt to paint him from memory. Since it's obvious that you can't work from life, use a good photograph of your setter. That's the least you can do for your pet to pay him back for the happy moments that he has given you.

Shetland Sheepdog

A herding dog, developed in the Shetland Islands, the sheltie has been sometimes called a miniature collie, but he is not; the breed is separate and distinct.

A sheltie's hair is long and silky, with assorted shades of color throughout. The following are mixtures to help you paint a sheltie in various shades of brown to almost white:

1. On the side of the dog away from the light, make a mixture of Burnt Umber, Burnt Sienna and a little Raw Sienna in a gray of Ivory Black and white. Paint this color wherever you see the deeper tones of color and in strokes that are consistent with hair.

2. In the chest area, where the hair is quite light, mix Ivory Black, white, Yellow Ochre and a touch of Raw Sienna to paint this entire area and the light areas on the face as well.

3. There are many little nuances of color throughout both the dark and light sides of the dog and these are best adjusted as you look at the dog. For example, the legs are a warm brown, a mixture of Yellow Ochre, white and just a tiny bit of Cadmium Orange, as are parts of the chest and face areas. All your strokes go on top of already painted areas showing a thick coat of hair, which shelties have.

4. Use white with a little Yellow Ochre to paint the lightest hair you see, adding darker darks with Burnt Umber and just a touch of Alizarin Crimson where you see it darkest.

5. The nose is painted with Ivory Black and just a bit of Alizarin Crimson, lightening it where the light strikes with white into this mixture (don't let it look purple). A highlight may be added by mixing the tiniest bit of Thalo Blue into white and applied sparingly.

6. You get the shine on the sheltie's coat by mixing the barest amount of Thalo Blue into white and painting it across the hair in just a few places where the light makes the hair shine and then carefully "combing" it through the hair with a dry soft brush.

All of your strokes go on top of already painted areas showing a thick coat of hair, which shelties have.

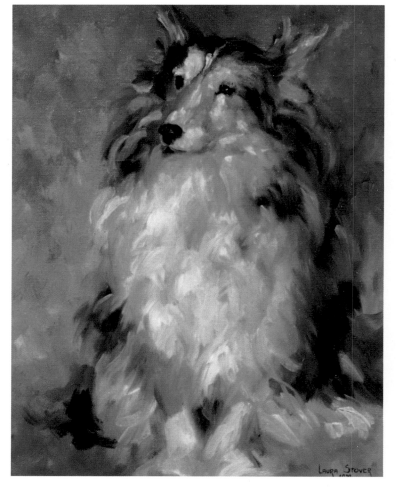

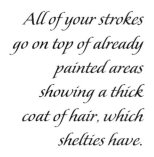

Helpful Hint: By applying your paint in strokes that indicate hair, the sheltie will take on a fluffy appearance and will look natural.

White Pony

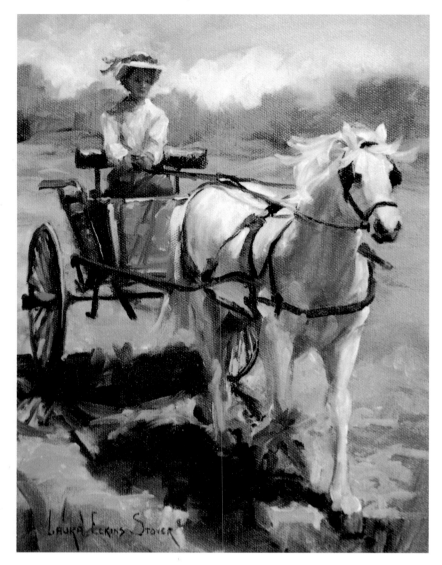

It's important to remember that everything that you paint is composed of the five tone values.

**The Carriage Fair, 9 x 12",
oil on canvas, Laura Elkins Stover,
*Private collection.***

People living in urban areas may not be too excited about painting this subject but in exurban communities and rural America in general, horses and ponies make popular subjects. We will deal here with a white pony hitched to a cart.

1. It's important to remember that everything that you paint — animate as well as inanimate — is composed of the five tone values, the elements that deliver three dimensions to your two-dimensional canvas. I guess you know by now that they are: the body tone, the body shadow, the cast shadow, highlight and reflection. Of course, they also show up in this white pony. The overall mixture for the pony is made with a warm gray: white, Ivory Black and Yellow Ochre.

2. Into this mixture add Raw Sienna and a bit of Cobalt Blue for the shadows, and in the deeper shadows, add a little Burnt Umber.

3. The lightest light is made with white and Yellow Ochre, adding more Yellow Ochre to this mixture as it turns into shadow and blends with the bluish tone.

4. The reflection in the underside of the neck and between the legs in shadow is made with respect to the area it is reflected from, in this case, it was made by adding just a touch of Thalo Yellow Green to the lightened version of the shadow color.

5. Highlighted areas are made by adding just the barest touch of Cerulean Blue to white and letting it glance across the lightest areas being careful not to overdo it.

Phlox

A characteristic of this flower is the loose and uneven way the individual blooms grow in the mass of the flower itself; it is a bit like the lilac in that respect. When painted to accentuate this feature, you will help it identify as a phlox. Colors of this flower range from deep rose to white. This Recipe will deal with the deep rose variety.

1. Into a mixture of Ivory Black and white, mix a little Alizarin Crimson and a touch of Thalo Red Rose. Paint the individual florets as you see them in the flowerhead.

2. Into the previous mixture, add Thalo Green and paint the petals that you see in shadow.

3. The petals on the light side will be painted with white and Thalo Red Rose. Where the light strikes the strongest, the color will be quite washed out, and in these cases, add more white to the mixture.

4. The very centers of some varieties are a deeper tone, and in this case it is Thalo Red Rose blended carefully at the center of each petal. Where the light strikes the hollow in the center it is much lighter; the lightest petal color may be added in this spot.

Helpful Hint: Indicating the way these individual florets grow from the main stem adds interest and charm to your painting. This may be done with fine strokes in a deep green color because most of these stems are shadowed by the blooms. Adding a few tiny buds is also attractive, and the same color mixtures can be used to accomplish this, being careful not to have them be too light.

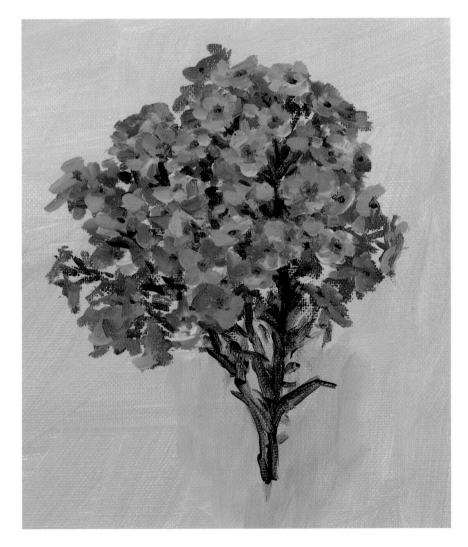

The characteristic of this flower is the loose and uneven way the individual blooms grow.

Delphinium

This tall and elegant flower comes in many colors, ranging from deep purple to white, and in single and double blooms. When painting a flower such as this, it is important to describe how each blossom grows from the stalk, including the unopened buds at the top; it adds charm and interest to the painting and further identifies the species. Since a medium blue delphinium seems to be a favorite, it is this color for which I will give the mixtures.

1. Mass each flower in with a darker blue than you see overall, and gray the color so that it will look natural and not too vibrant. Therefore, into a mixture of Ivory Black and white, add Ultramarine Blue and a speck of Alizarin Crimson; or Ultramarine Blue, Burnt Sienna, a touch of Alizarin Crimson and white. Paint this on your canvas with strokes that indicate petals and slightly larger than you see them, so you can cut it down with the background, and in that way end with the soft edges that are so important in this type of flower.

2. Mix more white into the previous mixture, and add a little more Alizarin Crimson in order to paint the mid-tone petals. Overlap them carefully to still see the mass tone between.

3. For the lightest petals, mix a little Cerulean Blue and a touch of Thalo Red Rose and white, painting only the lightest petals.

4. The very center of the bloom is quite dark and may be painted with Ivory Black, Alizarin Crimson and just a touch of white; paint this deep into the center. On top of this is a lighter part, and may be painted by mixing a light gray with Yellow Ochre, adding Raw Sienna to this mixture when the bloom is in shadow.

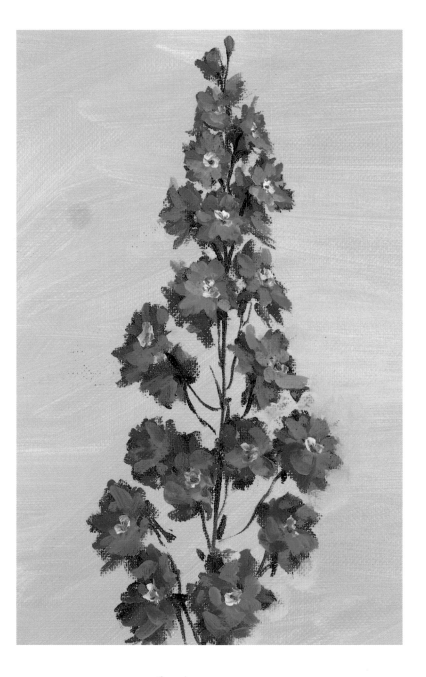

Helpful Hint: The unopened buds at the top of the stalk are sort of silvery in appearance. You can get this color by graying the blue mixture with Cadmium Orange and white.

Blue Hydrangea

In order to describe all the little florets in one hydrangea blossom, it is necessary to mass in the whole flower with a much deeper tone value than you see by squinting at the blossom. In this way, you can draw out the middle tone florets seen in the shadow side of the rounded bloom, and, then, the very light ones on the light side. The danger when painting these blue flowers is that you might get the color too vibrant. A way to stop this from happening is to mix all your colors into a gray made of Ivory Black and white, or by using the color's complement to gray it.

1. Mass in the entire bloom with a mixture of Ivory Black, white, Ultramarine Blue and just a touch of Burnt Umber. This should be painted showing the ragged edges of the blossom so that it doesn't look like just a rounded mass.

2. Mix a gray of Ivory Black and white, Ultramarine Blue and just a bit of Thalo Red Rose and indicate some of the petals you see on the shadowed side of the flower. Paint them in different positions to avoid repetition.

3. Into a mixture of Ivory Black and white, mix Cerulean Blue and a bit of Thalo Red Rose to paint the petals on the light side. Again, be careful to vary your strokes and also to leave some of the original mass tone peeking through. This mixture should be quite light, and can be lightened where the color is almost washed out by the sun.

Helpful Hint: Some of the petals on the shadowed side of the bloom will need to be lightened slightly from the original painting of them because they protrude from the blossom. Doing this will help show that the flower is beautifully round and full.

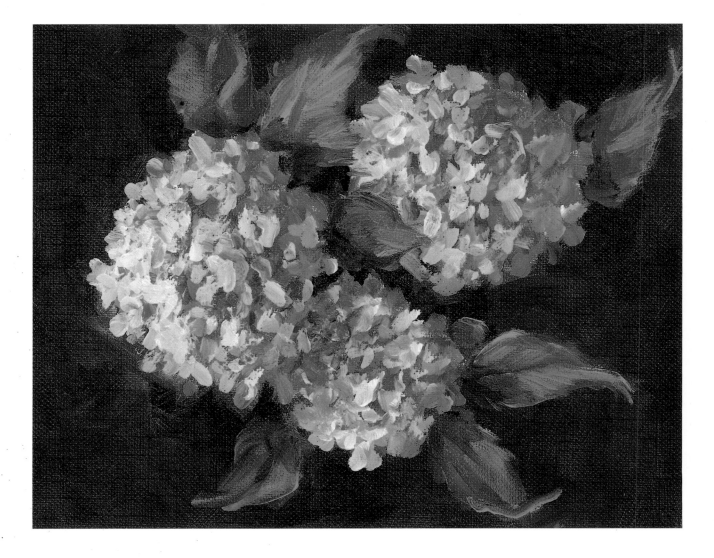

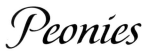

Peonies

A favorite flower in the summer garden, the peony comes in many shades of deep rose to creamy white. It is a spectacular blossom, and when successfully painted, it makes a lovely addition to a still life painting, or as a subject by itself.

Deep Rose Peony

1. Mass in the general shape of the peony in a mixture of Alizarin Crimson, Thalo Red Rose and a little white.

2. Add a little Ivory Black to this mixture to paint in the shadowed side of the peony.

3. Mix a little white into Thalo Red Rose to paint the petals on the light side of the peony.

White Peony

1. Mass in the general shape of the peony with a mixture of gray (Ivory Black and white) and Yellow Ochre (a warm gray).

2. Add a little more Ivory Black and a tiny bit of Alizarin Crimson to paint the shadowed side of the peony.

3. Paint the petals on the light side of the peony with a mixture of white and a little Yellow Ochre.

4. Most white peonies have a spot of red in the center. You can paint this with Grumbacher Red.

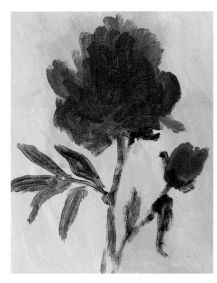

STEP 1.

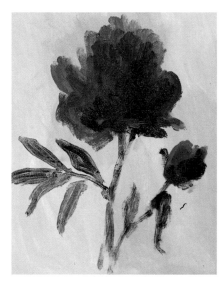

STEP 2.

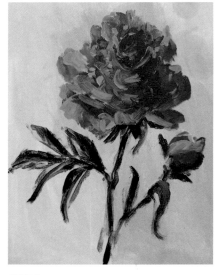

STEP 3.

Helpful Hint:

Keep the petals on the outer edges of the peonies soft by blending with the background. This helps to keep this large blossom looking round and dimensional

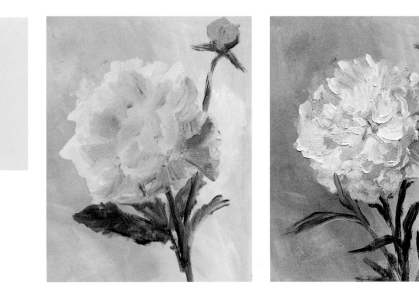

Drapery for Flower Picture

1. Arrange the drapery. Put the flowers in front of the drapes and notice how the folds touch the periphery of the bouquet. See that the folds lead into the vase rather than drape away out toward the edge of the picture. *REMEMBER:* The background should show off the subject and be in harmony with it.

2. See that there aren't any folds that are the same. The repetition of lines caused by folds is very much in opposition to the bouquet's shape.

3. See that the drape falls naturally down onto the table with some interesting patterns and that the vase seems to nestle in the drapery's surroundings.

4. Sketch on your canvas the silhouette of the bouquet even though, when painting the drapery, you'll overlap the drapery color into this shape.

5. Mass in the drapery color over the background area with short strokes, starting at the bouquet, not at the edges of the canvas.

6. To this tone add the color's complement to make a shadow color, and then paint the shadows in strokes that are opposite in direction from the lines in the folds.

7. Paint the cast shadow from the bouquet on the drape in the same short strokes you used to fill in the background.

8. You may accentuate the folds with some lighter tones, especially as the folds meet the bouquet.

To Sum Up: By painting the drapery in shorter strokes the rhythm of application will be more like the type of strokes you automatically use in painting flowers. And this factor seems to tie the whole painting together, which is so important to picture making.

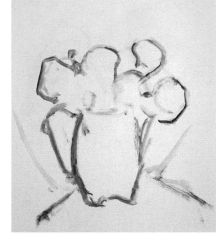

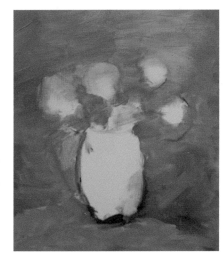

The background should show off the subject and be in harmony with it.

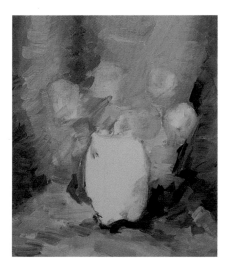

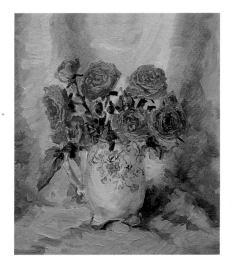

Helpful Hint:
Never paint in a large area with large strokes. A rhythm of many shorter strokes sets up a more interesting effect than the side-of-the-barn look that comes from large long strokes.

All-Important Background

No matter what kind of picture you paint you'll always have to paint a background. Make your backgrounds function as pleasant surroundings for your subjects by being aware of these questions each time you paint.

WHAT TONE DO I MAKE THE BACKGROUND?

For portraits, still lifes and florals a good way to decide what tone you want for the background is to set a large piece (at least 20" x 24") of first white and then black board behind the subject to determine whether it would look better against a light or dark background. *A Good General Rule* — light subjects need dark backgrounds; dark subjects need light backgrounds.

WHAT COLOR DO I MAKE THE BACKGROUND?

This is so much a matter of individual taste and isn't really as important as the tone of the background. I can say, however, that warm-colored backgrounds, like browns, dark orange, etc. give an earthier type of atmosphere.

The cool-colored backgrounds (like blue) present a more elegant effect. But no matter what color you use, *keep it in the background by graying it.* This can be done by mixing any color you want into a puddle of light gray for light backgrounds and into dark gray for dark ones.

SHOULD THE BACKGROUND BE BRIGHT OR DULL?

Brightly colored subject matter needs dull background colors. Conversely, any drab subject matter will need a brighter background to show it off.

SHOULD THE BACKGROUND BE SMOOTH OR ROUGH IN TEXTURE?

The background is often the first area that you paint. The look of it, then, will dictate how you're going to paint the rest of the picture. If you paint the background very smoothly you're committed to painting the rest of the picture the same way. Lay the background in with some brushstrokes showing a rhythm of application. This will give you more leeway in varying your brushstrokes when painting your subject matter.

SHOULD THE BACKGROUND HAVE ONE TONE VALUE THROUGHOUT?

Again, this is a matter of taste. A good rule: if you have a large area of background, you should have a variation of values. Usually, these tones should vary from light near the subject, to darker, toward the edges of the canvas.

No matter what color you make your background, incorporate that color's complement to make any shadows or any darker areas. For instance — a cast shadow from a copper pot on a yellowish green background would be a mixture of the yellowish green background plus Ivory Black and Alizarin Crimson to make a red violet that's complementary to the yellow green.

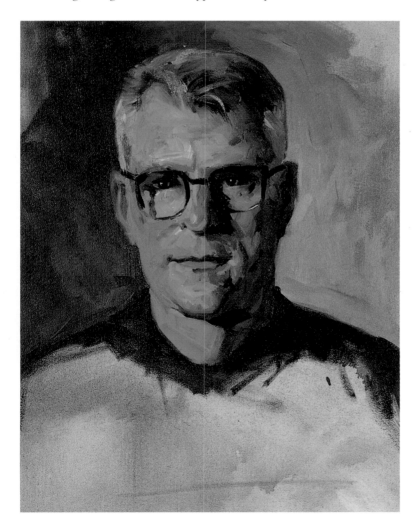

Big Sam, 20 x 24", oil on canvas.
The craggy virile face of my brother dictated the rough way the background would be painted.

Neck and Body of a Portrait

I've seen some beautifully painted faces sitting on top of tasteless, unconvincing necks and bodies. Whenever I see this I'm saddened, because I know why this had happened: the painter had put too much stress on a likeness instead of making a good painting and a presentation of the model's countenance. This mistake, then, is a result of neglect rather than lack of ability.

The neck and body of a portrait are harder to paint than the face. They're relegated to playing supporting roles. Here are some practical disciplines to help you make the lower half of your portrait support the good likeness that you've gotten in a better way:

1. When you work on the face, don't stop at the chin. Continue your painting process of the skin area down, even beyond the clothing line.

2. Carefully observe how the clothing casts shadows on the skin, and record them softly.

3. Make sure the color of the garment doesn't fight with the skin or background color.

4. Don't paint the body color until your background color is painted far into the body area. It's also a good idea to use the background color that's near the canvas edge to cover the bottom area of the canvas. This makes it possible for you to start at the collar line — whatever shape it is — and have this color meet and mix in with the background color which will make the body fade away at the bottom. It's far better than having the body look flat and pasted on and sitting on the bottom edge of the frame.

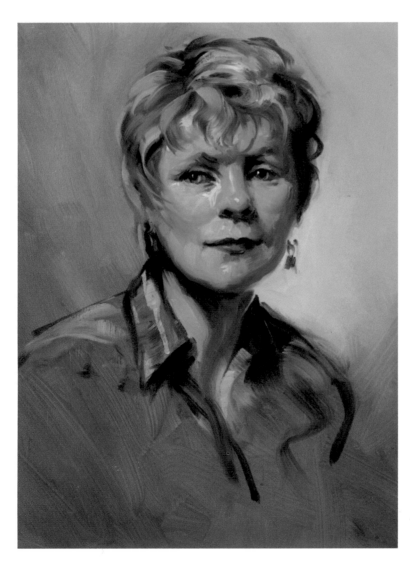

Don't paint the body color until your background color is painted far into the body area.

String of Pearls

To add a string of pearls to a still life or a portrait it's best to do it on a surface that's dry. If the surface isn't dry — use a "Q-Tip," and moisten with turpentine to "draw in" a line where the pearls are to be. Observe how perspective alters the look of the strand. Those pearls that are right in line with your eyes are round and completely visible. As they turn away from — or toward — your line of vision, one pearl overlaps another.

After the entire strand has been sketched, mass in each pearl, starting with the largest and ending with the smallest (if the pearls are graduated in size).

MASS TONE COLOR: Pearls are usually a warm gray: Burnt Umber into Ivory Black and white; or Venetian Red into Ivory Black and white, since pearls are quite often pinkish. Now, instead of using black and white, the gray color for the mass tone can be a mixture of a color and its complement, such as Cadmium Red Light, Chromium Oxide Green, and white; or Raw Sienna, Manganese Violet, and white. No matter which way you do it, make sure the initial value of your pearls is dark enough to enable you to use white with a little touch of Yellow Ochre as a highlight. This is the only way the pearls will appear to glow.

NEVER put this highlight in the middle of each pearl. Instead, place the highlight one-third in of the edge of the pearl that's closest to the light. Also — place it higher than the middle. Put this highlight on the pearl in a rather thick mixture so it "stands up" in a peak. With a clean dry brush, touch this mound of highlight paint and ease it onto the mass tone. If this process has blended the highlight too much, plop the highlight on again.

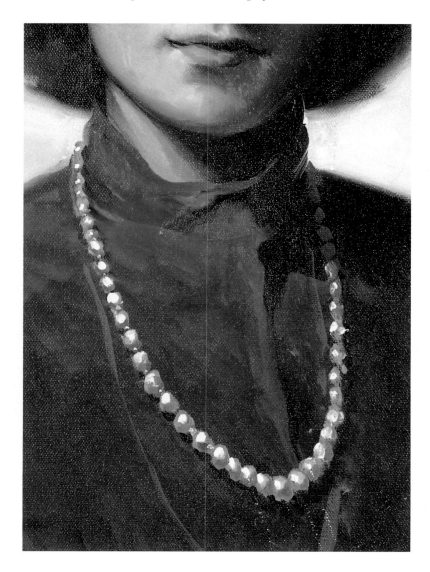

THE SHADOWS: With a mixture of a violet that's a few shades darker than the mass tone (Alizarin Crimson and a breath of Thalo Green into the mass tone) paint the little shadows that you see on the one-third portion of the pearls that's going away from the light. This shadow's often shaped like a crescent.

THE CAST SHADOW: from each pearl helps to set the string down on the table (if painted in that setting) or will give the pearls dimension as they grace a woman's neck.

SHADOW COLOR ON SKIN: Ivory Black and white, Venetian Red, and a little Yellow Ochre.

SHADOW COLOR ON A TABLE: Thalo Blue, Burnt Umber. *The reflections are very important.* They're quite light because one pearl reflects another. They can be almost as light as the highlight. Mix by putting a little Burnt Umber or Burnt Sienna into white. On a woman's skin, this reflection is often Venetian Red and white.

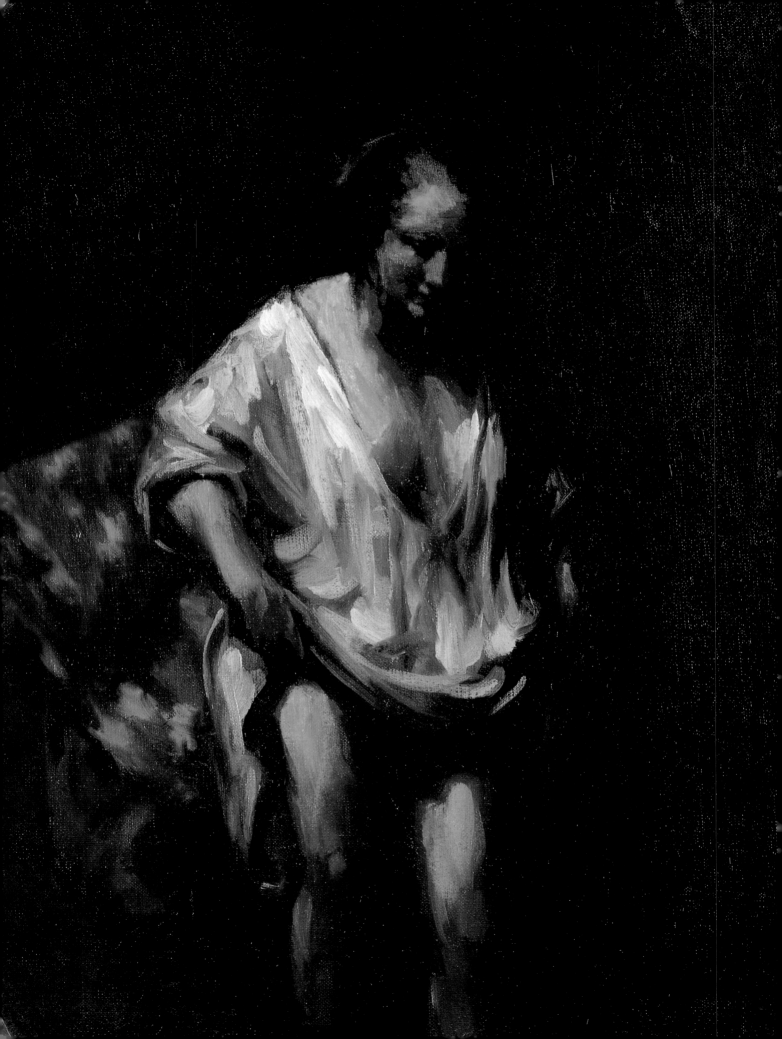

Copying From the Masters

Among the many ways a painter can study is to copy pictures that were painted by artists of the past. After all, you can't paint a good picture until you've seen a good picture.

Obviously, the easiest and least expensive way to copy your favorite painter is from reproductions in the many art books that are available in book stores and public libraries. You will find, however, that following this course may not be all that desirable since the quality of color printing may vary from publisher to publisher. If an art museum is not easily in reach, you would have no choice but to work from the paintings as they appear in the aforementioned books.

Copying the original paintings right in the museums is such a rewarding experience that you should try to make an effort to do so. I did the painting "A Woman Bathing" to study Rembrandt's free style of painting. I learned that his seemingly *alla prima* technique must surely have been painted onto a preliminary plan which makes such a spontaneous technique have so much form and solidity.

Rembrandt's masterpiece hangs in the National Gallery in London. I painted it on one of my visits to the English capital. The original is approximately 18½" by 24⅜". I made my copy 11¼" by 15¼", about a sixty percent reduction. All museums, you will find, require a reduction of at least ten percent. The reason is obvious, and is flattering to the skills of the copyist that the finished copy could ever be mistaken for the original.

I suggest that you check with your local museum for the guidelines that they have surely set down in order for you to be able to copy any painting from their collection.

I have written to three major museums in the country to learn from them what they require artists to do if they plan to do any copying on the museums' premises. Here's what they sent me:

The Metropolitan Museum of Art, New York

1. Each copyist must provide and work with a drop cloth.
2. Paint, palette, canvases and other equipment must never be left unattended in the galleries.
3. Canvases must not exceed 30" x 30"; they must differ from the original in size by at least ten percent.
4. Only one copyist at a time may work in a gallery.

Museum of Fine Arts, Boston

1. Works on loan to the museum cannot be copied.
2. Copying may be done only in the galleries, not in corridors.
3. An adequate drop cloth or paper must be supplied by the copyist.
4. Copies must vary by at least ten percent in height and width from the original.
5. Copies in watercolors and acrylics are not permitted.

National Gallery of Art, Washington, D.C.

Individuals wishing to copy must present the following: Two letters of character reference; two letters of reference regarding artistic proficiency; two samples of the applicant's painting (color transparencies or slides are not acceptable substitutes); suitable identification — current driver's license, bank book or passport. If, after all of this, you still want to go ahead with the project, here are the copying rules:

1. The size of the copy material must be at least two inches smaller or two inches larger than each of the dimensions of the original canvas.
2. Only one copyist at a time is permitted to work in a gallery.
3. Easels must be placed no closer than four feet from the painting being copied.
4. The use of spray fixatives is prohibited.
5. If the original artist's signature is also copied, it must bear with it the copyist's name and date and the words: "Copy after..."

Miniatures

Miniatures date back to the 17th century and, perhaps, even earlier. From the 18th century on, transparent watercolors were used almost exclusively, while before then, tempera and other painting media were used. Today, there has been a rebirth of painting small pictures on small surfaces, with a number of miniature painting societies actively exhibiting the works of their many members.

According to the eligibility requirements of most of these societies, original works submitted may not exceed 7" x 9", including the frame, with a maximum of 25 square inches of painted area.

An artist working in miniature has several choices of grounds to work on: Ivorine, an artificial ivory; fine grained canvas; parchment paper that has been carefully sealed; and any fine and sturdy paper which has been primed and is acid free.

The artist applies paint in very thin layers and in tiny strokes, allowing each application to dry before applying subsequent layers. Between layers, it is useful to rub gently with a very fine steel wool to eliminate brushstrokes which may show, and to gently rub in a little medium to restore the original luster before continuing with other layers.

Brushes made of sable or imitation sable are best, with sizes 0 to 1 working very well. When painting miniatures, the use of a magnifying glass is a big help, especially one mounted on a stand, thus leaving both hands free. Most miniature art clubs provide magnifying glasses at their exhibitions to make it easier for visitors to view the many paintings.

Victorian Lady, Laura Elkins Stover, oil on canvas.
Shown here in actual size.

Composition

The composition of a picture is its linear design; it's the placement of elements in a painting which forms the very foundation over which the bricks and mortar of drawing, value, texture and color will be built. This is the design of the subject on the canvas; it's an arrangement to pictorialize the subject, first in delineated design, then with form, contrast and color.

At this time, drawing is still a premature involvement. Leave the drawing until later when you want to define the shapes you deal with. Composition merely indicates where the shapes are going to be. It charts the direction of the shapes, but does not delineate the actual shapes. You can't rush the painting process; first things must come first. Doing any intricate drawing at the compositional stage will only speed you away from this important element.

As an exercise, I used to ask my students to compose a still life that I set up in front of them. After thirty seconds, I'd say, "Stop," and they would all groan. No one was finished because each student had become involved with drawing, not with composition.

In this section of the book, I will acquaint you (or, in many cases, re-acquaint you) with the basic elements of making a design for your painting.

The *placement* of the elements in the painting is the start of the design, indicated on the canvas with but a few well-placed marks.

The *focal point* (known also as the center of interest) directs the viewer's eye to a point in the painting that the artist has artistically arranged to best decorate the motivation, which, after all, is the reason for the painting in the first place.

Within the framework of the overall plan, there has to be *balance*, *unity* and *variety* for the painting to be of interest to anyone viewing it.

And, of course, an important help to the artist is the *contrast of the light and dark patterns* in the picture.

What is a Still Life?

A still life is an arrangement of forms that combine to present a pictorial story, a mood or a recollection of a visual experience. The composition of a still life should be a sound design, one that has balance, unity and variety. In pictorial expression, the design always has a focal point. This is often called the "center of interest," which is never in the center of the canvas.

A. By doing an abstraction of our still life, we can find the picture's overall composition. This is more important than a record of the subject's realism.

B. In this diagram of our still life, the "X" points out the center of interest. The arrows show how your eye is led in the direction around and toward the center of interest rather than away from it. *IMPORTANT:* One focal point per picture! Don't paint anything that will rob it of its importance.

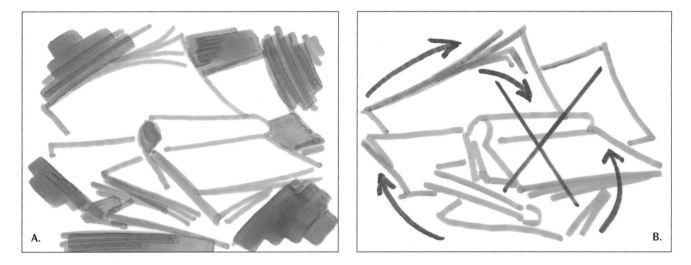

A.

B.

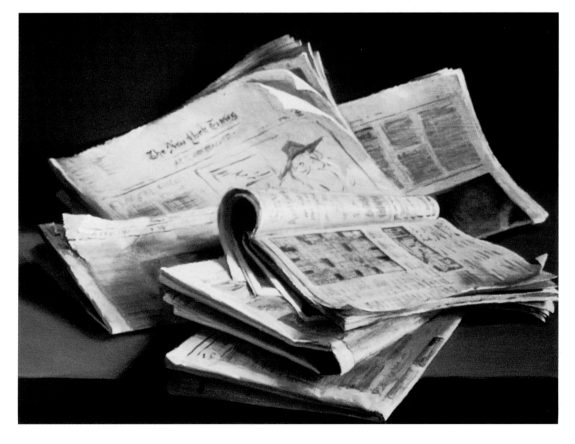

The Importance of Placement

When you begin a still life, never start by drawing the objects. Instead, place marks at the top, bottom, left and right sides of the canvas to indicate the outer edges of the entire composition. This practice helps you to make the arrangement fit the size of your canvas. If you begin by drawing one of the objects (a very common mistake), you'll never be in control of your arrangement on the canvas.

Here's How you Should Begin the Two Pictured Still Lifes

Composition is more of an initial factor in picture making than is drawing. Don't try to compose and draw simultaneously. The drawing only further defines the many shapes that make up the composition.

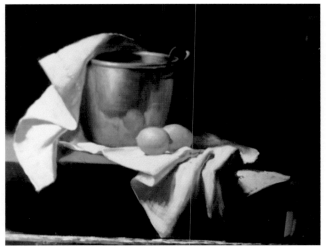

STILL LIFE 1.

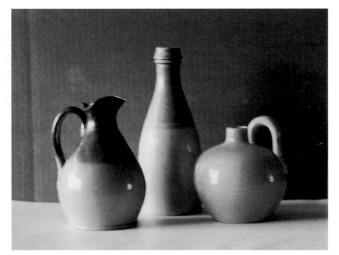

STILL LIFE 2.

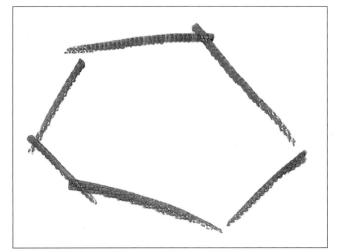

COMPOSITION 1.

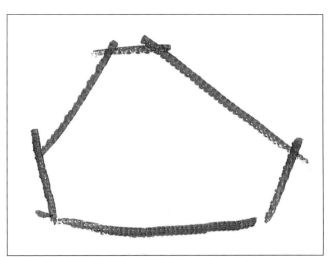

COMPOSITION 2.

The Factors of Unity
& Variety in Composition

We enjoy *variety* rather than monotony. Avoid making your compositions monotonous by using uneven numbers of forms that aren't the same size and aren't evenly spaced. At the same time, however, your picture must also have a feeling of *unity*. Unity is a matter of making the still life look like a plausible circumstance. You get unity by combining objects and shapes that are allied, and then painting the picture in a consistent manner.

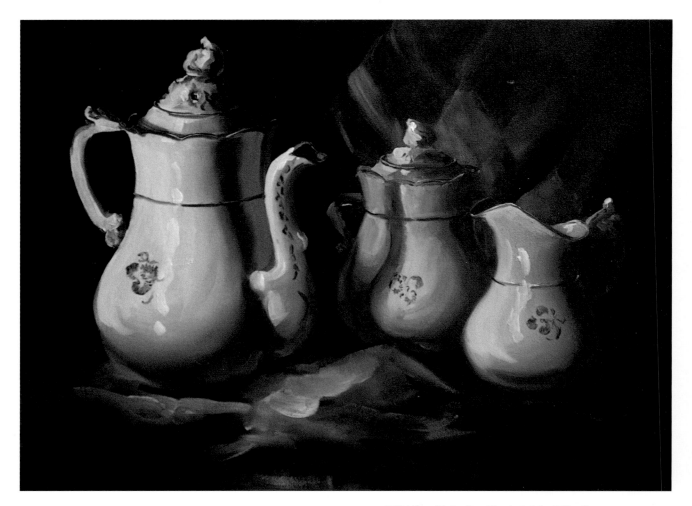

Still Life with Indian Blanket, 16 x 20", oil on canvas, Laura Elkins Stover, *Private collection.*

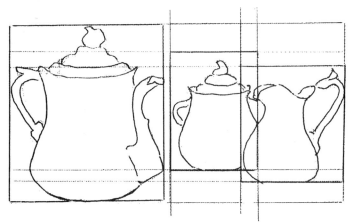

Lines show that no objects are the same width, nor do they fall in line with each other in height.

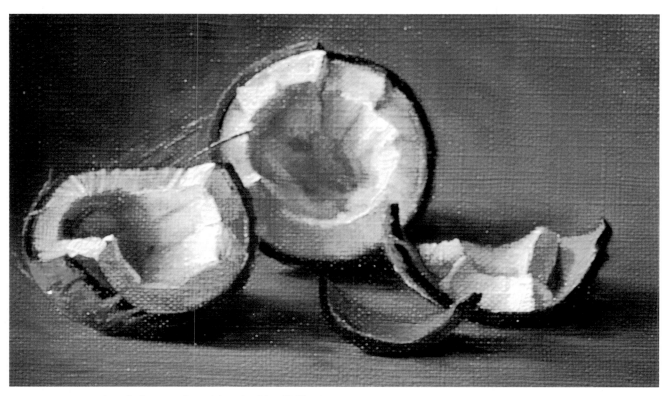

STILL LIFE A. Even though there are four objects in this still life, there are only three masses — the white meat of the coconut. Furthermore, each white area is a different shape and a different size. Don't be afraid to make exceptions.

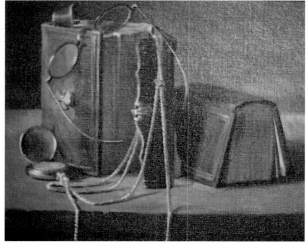

STILL LIFE B. Your overall composition should more often be shaped triangularly. Designing an arrangement that forms a square or a rectangle will repeat the shape of the canvas. Avoid this kind of repetition.

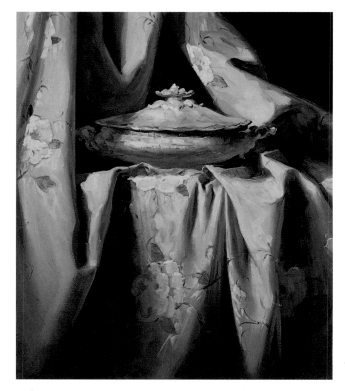

STILL LIFE C. This picture of a soup tureen points out unity and variety. Its unity is the quiet mood throughout; its variety is the contrast of the round shape of the pot with the angles and rectangle of the napkin and tablecloth.

The Factor of Balance in Composition

Balance is a factor in nature. We ask our pictures to also have balance in order for them to look natural. Balance, then, means that the center of interest has to be held up by the secondary forms of the composition.

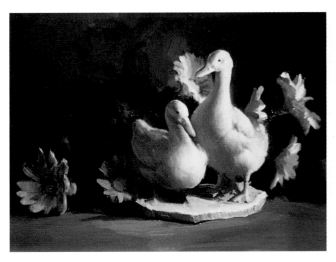

STILL LIFE A. The porcelain geese and the flowers that are placed near them are balanced by the flower on the table at the lower left corner.

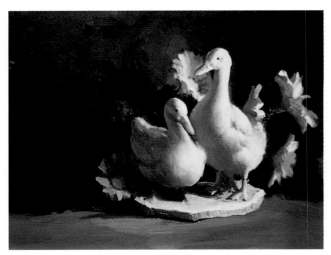

STILL LIFE B. With the flower on the table removed, there's no feeling of balance.

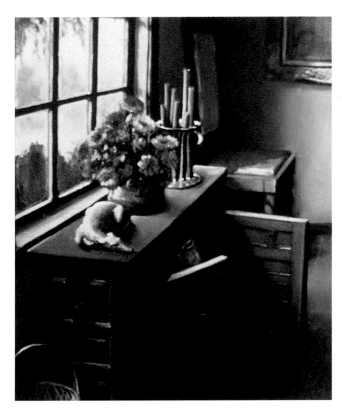

STILL LIFE C. The bouquet of flowers (focal point) is balanced by the painting which hangs on the wall in the upper right of the composition.

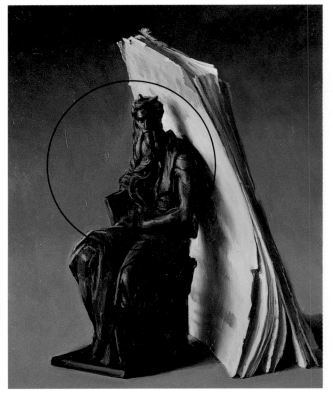

STILL LIFE D. The focal point — or center of interest — is not an object; it's a place. It is indicated by a circle.

The Basic Still Life Composition

A basic still life composition is an arrangement of objects that are different in size, form a triangle and are related to each other. A successful still life is a picture of a universal truth, which means a mood or a pictorial incident that's recognizable to everyone.

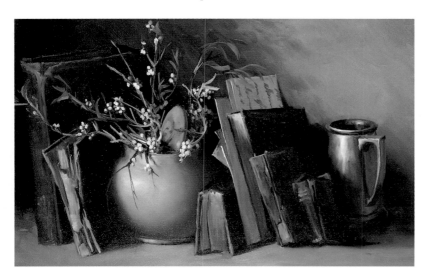

Don't paint what the object is, paint what the object's all about.

STILL LIFE A. There are ten objects in this picture, but the way they're arranged presents an uneven feeling of masses. You'll find three round shapes, books that form a triangle, and books that form a rectangle. The round shapes surround the bulk of the books, holding them in the picture.

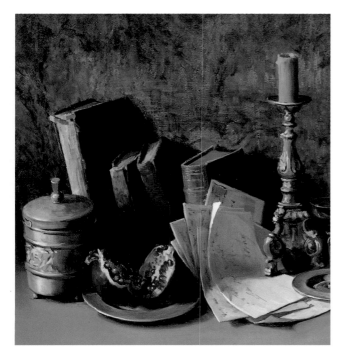

STILL LIFE B. While many people may not be familiar with the canister on the left, everyone will know that it's made of brass because it shines. The shine, then, is the universal truth, not the canister itself.

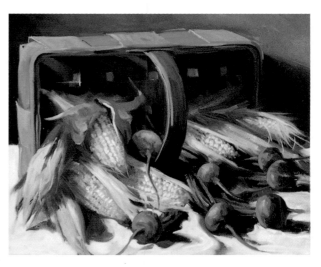

STILL LIFE C. This picture is different because the more agitated tone values of shucks and corns surround the center of interest, which is the cluster of red beets.

Contrast of Light & Dark Patterns in Composition

It's obvious that still lifes are made up of objects, but their compositions are more a matter of the light and dark patterns that are caused by the objects. Lighting, therefore, becomes very important, since contrasts are caused by your lighting. And the best contrasts are caused by one source of light, just as in nature.

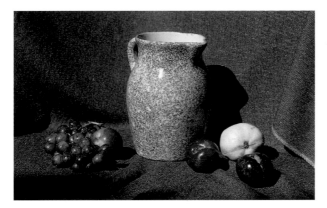 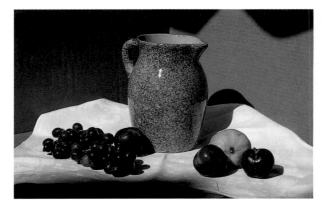

COMPOSITION A. The relatively flat lighting in the picture on the left doesn't show off the three-dimensional quality of the objects. The photo on the right shows how a lighter table has made the shapes of the fruit more important and the stronger lighting has made the ceramic pot shine and look more round. The entire composition now has a more unified look.

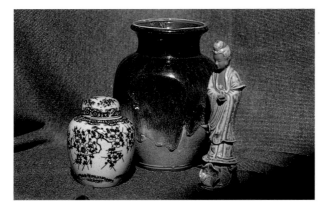 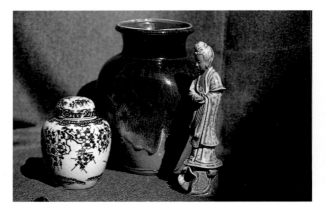

COMPOSITION B. Notice how the improved lighting (on the right) has made the statue stand away from the vase because it casts a shadow on the vase. The cast shadow from the large vase shows off the smaller vase's shape more gracefully.

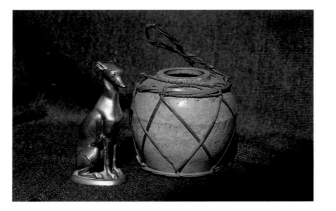 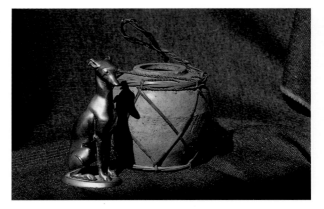

COMPOSITION C. The lighting on the statue of the dog in the picture on the right defines the statue's shape much better than the confusing lighting on the left. *IMPORTANT:* Don't paint what the object is, paint what the lighting does to it!

Helpful Hints About Composition

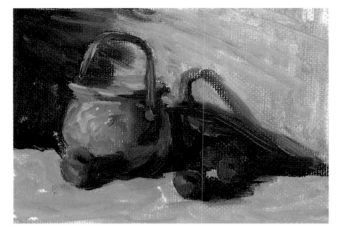

COMPOSITION A. Use your cast shadow pattern to tie your composition together.

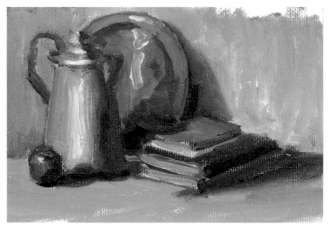

COMPOSITION B. Something can be in the middle as long as the something isn't the focal point.

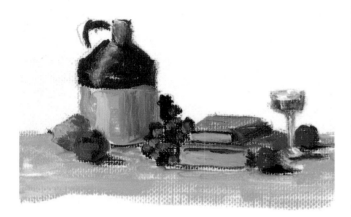

COMPOSITION C. Always have the more unusual shape among a group of things placed toward the center of the composition and flanked by the more repetitious shapes.

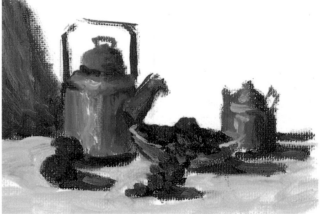

COMPOSITION D. Any object that's going in a definite direction, such as spouts on teapots, lips of pitchers, etc., should lead into the picture.

Rights & Wrongs in Still Life

The three painted diagrams on the left have all been intentionally designed with errors in composition. These errors have been corrected in the three still lifes that appear on the right.

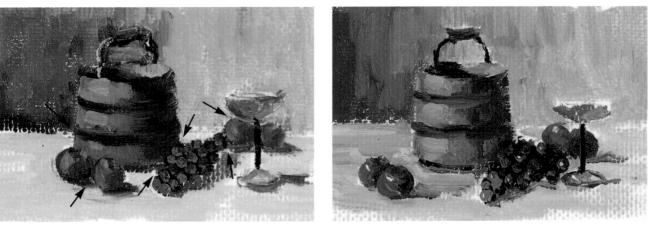

STILL LIFE A. Don't let objects just touch. Overlap them or separate them.

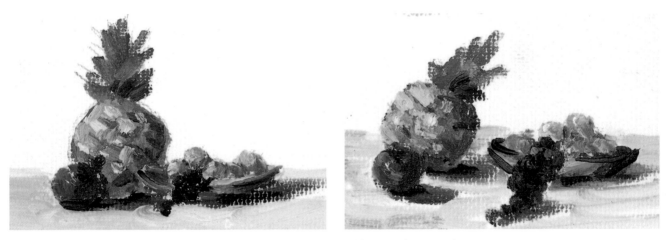

STILL LIFE B. Don't put all your objects on the same plane.

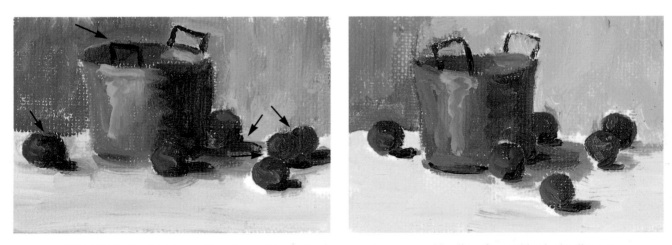

STILL LIFE C. Don't let the outline of something in the foreground converge with a line of something in the distance, or — as you've heard so often from me — don't let them "kiss."

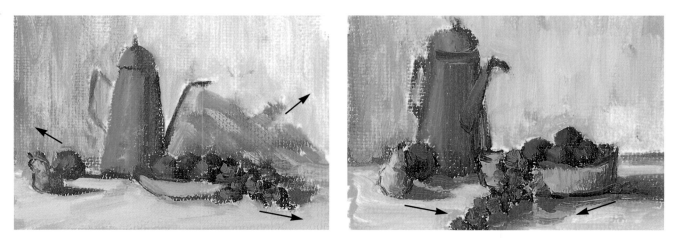

STILL LIFE D. Don't let anything lead you out of the picture.

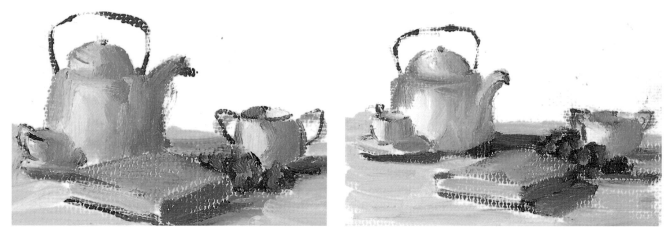

STILL LIFE E. Don't let anything just touch the edges of the canvas.

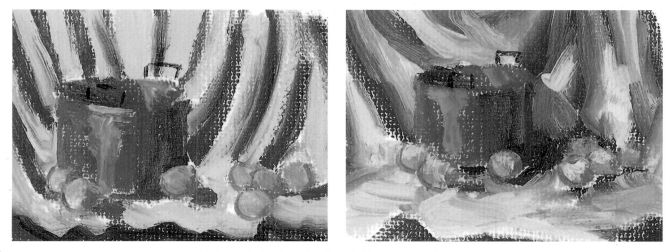

STILL LIFE F. Don't make all the folds in drapery the same.

"It's Not What You Paint...

Fine statement, but it doesn't solve the problem of WHAT TO PAINT! Here's my list of suggestions that should open your eyes to the interesting still lifes you could make from the many things around your home:

1. Apples. Place some closer to you and some farther back to form the composition. Group some together, have others stand alone. Place them on a white cloth or on a shiny table. Use any other fruit or vegetable.

2. Group a collection of old crocks or a bunch of old bottles.

3. Arrange cooking utensils, such as a copper pot, a black skillet, etc., with vegetables. Fruits are better arranged with teapots, wine bottles, and any other object that's associated with eating rather than with cooking.

4. A pile of books alone or with a brass ashtray, a candle stick and a glass of wine.

5. Many things can be combined with a wicker basket: eggs, balls of yarn, seashells, fruits or vegetables.

6. Try hanging some things from a nail or hook in the wall. An old lantern, musical instruments, some chianti bottles, are some items that you can use.

7. Some clay flower pots present a colorful challenge. Save any that may break; they make provocative subjects.

8. Oriental things, such as a little Chinese or Japanese statue and a spice jar. Place them in front of a brass tray.

9. Any arrangement of items used for jobs such as sewing, painting, crocheting, writing, carpentry, etc.

A Word of Caution: Don't paint anything that's very unusual. Make your arrangements as natural looking as possible. Most often an inspiration for a still life comes from a visual experience. You see something and it intrigues you to paint a picture that says, "This is how it looks to me." Sure this makes you have to search out stuff. But for a still life painter that's part of the fun.

After reading this list, you will no doubt wonder why flowers haven't been presented here since floral arrangements make such "paintable" subject matter. Flower pictures are such a unique and special type of still life painting that only a separate book can do them any justice. In fact, I have written a flower painting instruction book. *Painting Flowers the Van Wyk Way* is a comprehensive treatment of the subject. It is published by Art Instruction Associates and distributed by North Light Books.

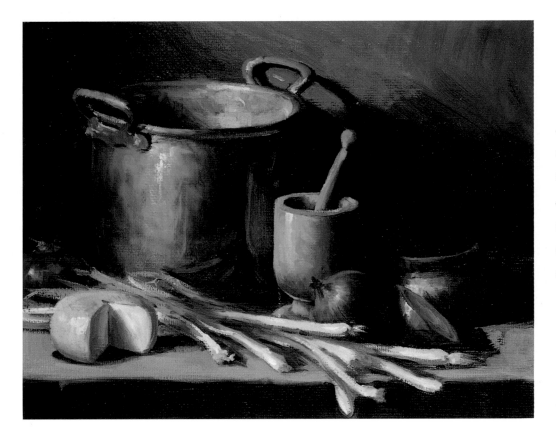

Don't paint anything that's very unusual. Make your arrangements as natural looking as possible.

But How You Paint It."

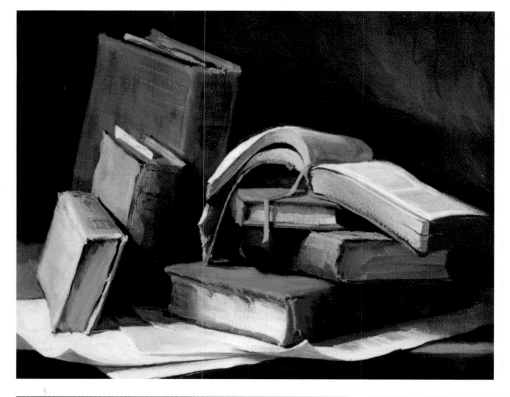

Most often an inspiration for a still life comes from a visual experience.

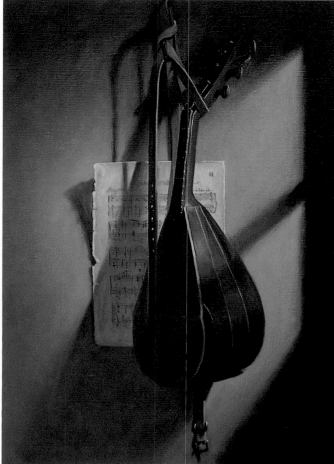

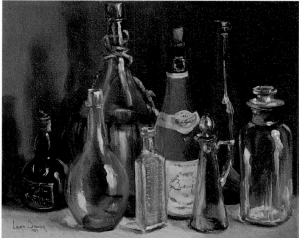

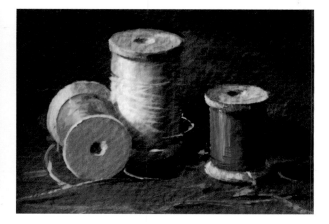

The Importance of Backgrounds

This may seem strange to you, but the background is the hardest part of the still life to paint. In color, in value, and in manner of application, the background should complement the subject matter and not detract from it. The background is the area that records the subjects' atmosphere or surroundings, and thus it creates the entire mood of the picture.

Tips About Backgrounds

1. Always start painting your background from the middle of the picture and work out towards the edges of the canvas. The reason: the color can be darkened and more muted around the edges to help frame the interest in the center of the picture. The true color of the background, then, will be near the subject matter.

2. Paint your background in a manner of application that will be consistent with the subject matter. *Example:* Don't paint your background roughly when your objects have been recorded smoothly.

3. Be careful of the color of your background. You're much safer with grayed background colors than with bright background colors.

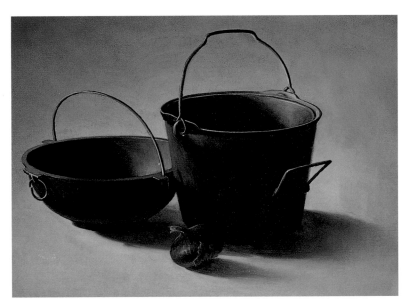

STILL LIFE A. Dark subject matter — light background.
Light subject matter — dark background

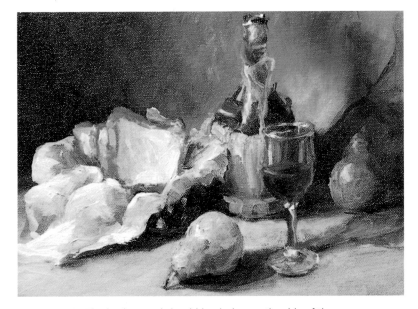

**Still Life with Bread,
9 x 12", oil on canvas,
Laura Elkins Stover,
*Private collection.***

*Don't paint your background
roughly when your objects
have been recorded smoothly.*

STILL LIFE B. The background should be darker on the side of the canvas where the light comes from.

Procedure

*I*n every field of endeavor, workers find ways to do their jobs more efficiently to make better products for us. Following systems that have been set up before them, and coming up with new ones on their own, they manage to bring this about more easily. Nothing of any value is just turned out in a helter-skelter manner. Everything that's created, everything that's manufactured, is done so by way of a set of procedures.

Creating works of art should be no different. The artists of old understood this; they were a disciplined lot. They couldn't have produced so much were it not for a procedural plan that each and every one of them used in one way or another.

As a painter, you follow a certain routine once you are aware of what you are going to paint. You're concerned with the many factors of the painting process: the painting surface you want to paint on, the paints and colors that you will use, the brushes to apply those paints, the mediums for you to mix with the paints and, finally, the frame you will choose to adorn the finished painting. The most important tool you should be using from the very first stroke is not on the list. It is common sense, which will dictate a practical way to paint your picture.

If you have been painting for any length of time, maybe you have become aware of how much your common sense is involved in the scores of decisions you are called upon to make during the course of even one painting. If you're new to the craft of painting, believe me when I say that many of the problems that you will run into can be solved by just thinking them out. I have written books, given demonstrations and taught painting for years in order to pass on to my students the basic fundamentals: materials, color mixing theory, hints about drawing and proportion, and composition. Within the framework of teaching the fundamentals, my philosophy and my personal way of painting is laced with a wealth of procedures — some call them "studio hints"— that have worked for me and for the people who have flown under my teacher's wing.

In this section of the book, I will let you in on the practical approach to the business of "manufacturing" a painting. Once you have read it, and, even *more* important, once you have tried it, you will be able to see the logic behind organizing your painting in this fashion. So, let's get started.

A Basic Procedure

The most practical approach to painting a landscape, portrait or still life is to start with the area that's most distant from you, and then progressively paint each thing or plane as it comes closer to you.

Fountain in the Pincio, Rome

1. The trees in the background and their values were painted in first.
2. The light on the ground behind the fountain was next.
3. The fountain, pedestal and pool came next.
4. The water spraying upward and falling over the edge were painted next. The area in step 1 had to be dry in order for this light value to be dragged on.
5. The tree in the foreground was added last, along with lighter lights and shadows on the ground.

Rockport Child

1. After sketching in the child's position with the chair, the background was toned.
2. The child's face, hair and neck were painted.
3. The sleeves, collar and dress followed.
4. Since she was leaning on the chair, that had to be done next.
5. Finally, the arms were the last to be painted.

Study of Books

1. After the composition was planned, the background and cast shadow were painted in first.
2. The book in the back is next to be painted.
3. The two books — on the right and on the left — are added along with the cast shadow from the book on the right.
4. The bottom book, lying on the table, is next to be added.
5. Resting on top of the book in #4, the open book with the lifted leaf is painted.
6. The tabletop is the last to be painted.

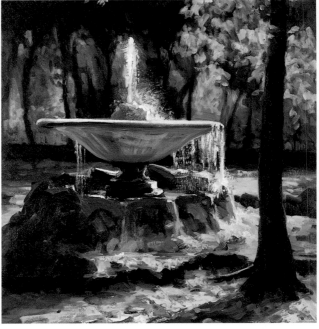

Fountain in the Pincio, Rome, 20 x 24", *Private Collection*

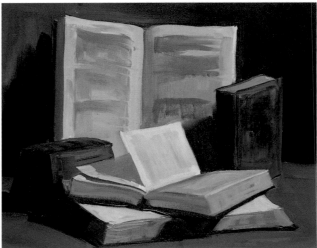

Study of Books, 20 x 24", *Private Collection*

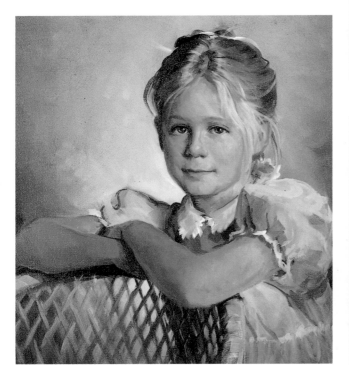

Rockport Child, 16 x 16", *Private Collection*

Making the Basic Procedure Work

This basic procedure is a starting point that can be varied at your own discretion. But it's a good rule of thumb to start from the back and come forward: sky before mountain; shirt before coat; or anything that seems to be in back of something else.

Here's a step-by-step progression showing how working from far to near enables you to overlap one area over another. This produces a so-called line which, in painting, is really one tone bumped up against another contrasting one.

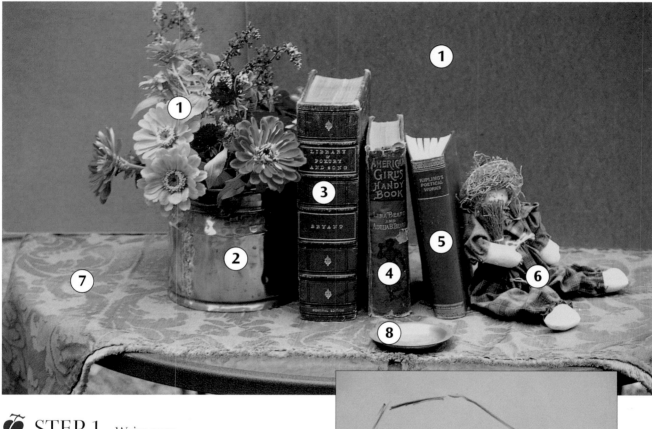

🍂 STEP 1. We've numbered each element in the still life, starting with #1 — the most distant — and ending with #8 — the closest — to show you the progression of application. 1. Background, including shadows of the books and flowers and the flowers themselves as far as the top of the copper bucket. 2. The bucket and flowers that overlap it. 3. The first book. 4. The second book. 5. The third book. 6. The little straw doll. 7. The tabletop. 8. The brass ashtray.

🍂 STEP 2. *The Placement.* I can't stress enough the importance of designating how large your arrangement's going to be on the canvas. *REMEMBER:* the size of your canvas is the only thing you know about your painting at this time. You must adjust your subject matter to it.

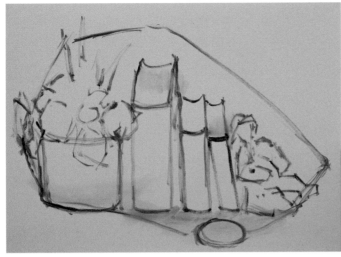

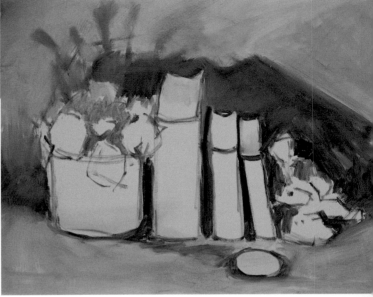

🍃 **STEP 4.** *The Basic Lay-in of Tones.* This can be done by using a dark tone such as Burnt Umber or Ivory Black (greatly thinned, of course) for the dark areas and leave the white canvas for the light areas.

🍃 **STEP 3.** *The Drawing.* These are the necessary lines to crystallize in your mind what the picture's going to look like in the end. Realize that these lines will be covered in the painting process.

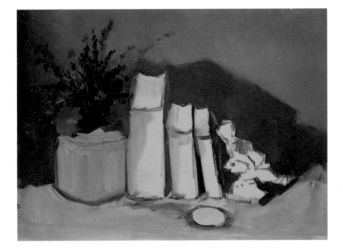

🍃 **STEP 5.** *The Procedure Begins.* This shows that the background has been painted in, including the shadows from the books and flowers, and the flowers themselves as far as the top of the copper bucket.

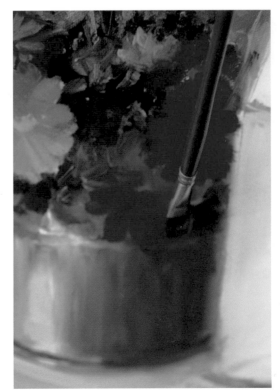

🍃 **STEP 6.** Next, the bucket and the blossoms over-lapping it were painted.

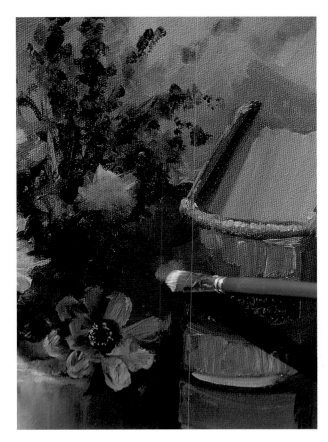

🍂 STEP 7. The large
book has been painted, and the
flowers which overlap it were added.

🍂 STEP 8. The second
book is painted, cutting into the
first book and overlapping the third.

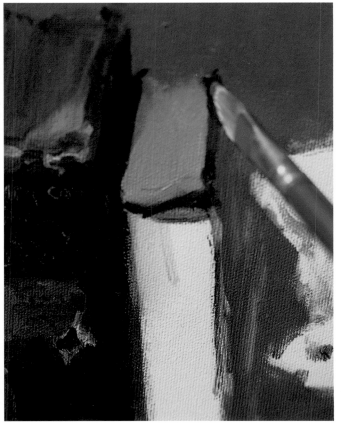

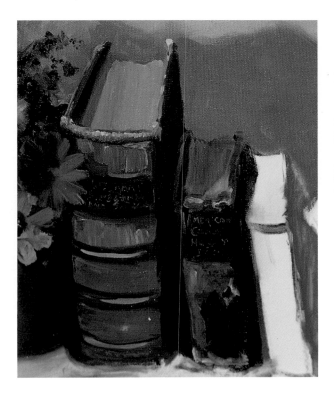

🍂 STEP 9. At this point,
the third book is painted against the
second book.

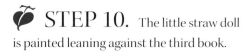 **STEP 10.** The little straw doll is painted leaning against the third book.

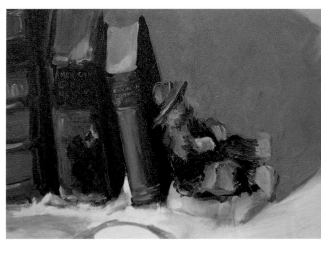

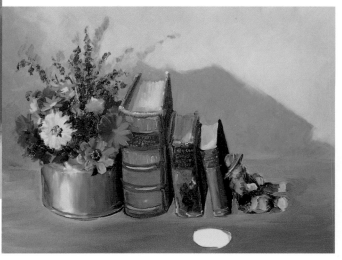

STEP 11. The tabletop is painted in an overall tone, to be worked on later.

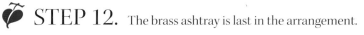 **STEP 12.** The brass ashtray is last in the arrangement.

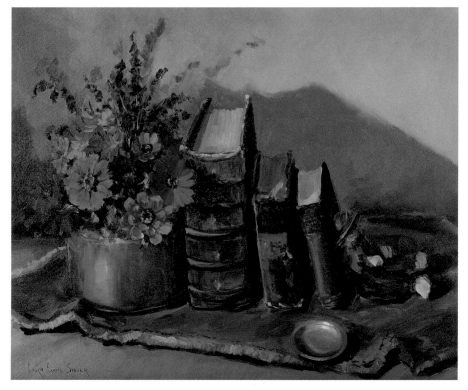

Books and Zinnias, 18 x 24", *by Laura Elkins Stover.*

STEP 13.

The Finished Painting. This step illustrates how all the objects are constructed with light and dark, and how the tones meet carefully and accurately because of the progression of application just described. You can see how substantial your groundwork has to be, because from here on in it's just a matter of accentuation not a matter of structure. Darker darks and lighter lights have been added and the scarf was put into the foreground for interest.

REMEMBER: extend the first thing you paint so the next thing you paint can overlap it! And, finally — the art of painting is how easy you do it. No one cares how much you suffer!

How to Blend the Edges of Shadows

In this detail of one of my paintings, you can see the strong contrasts that are caused by the lighting. *REMEMBER:* you can't paint a feeling of dimension without seeing contrasts of light and dark. You can only make your paint record what the light does to the subject. Your paint can be a physical substitute for light, never a substitute for things such as trees, skin or vases. You only see your subject because the light is showing it up. So paint the effect of light and make your pictures look dimensional and luminous.

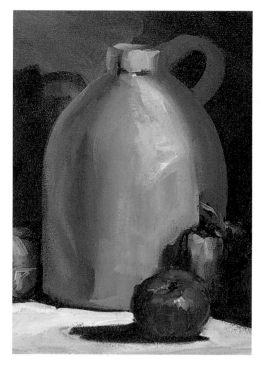

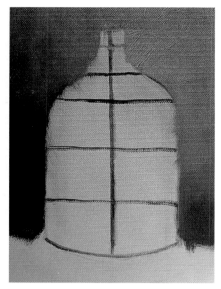

🌰 **STEP 1.** Start out with some guide lines.

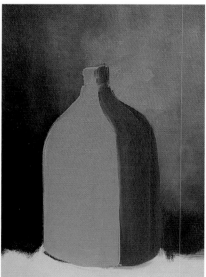

🌰 **STEP 2.** Lay in the shadow and basic tone, being concerned only with the shapes of each.

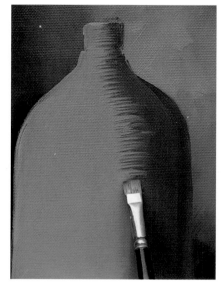

🌰 **STEP 3.** Now, with one half of a dry brush on the light side and the other half of the brush on the shadow side, wiggle your brush as you move it down the shadow's edge. A size 14 Red Sable Bright (short length) is ideal for this maneuver.

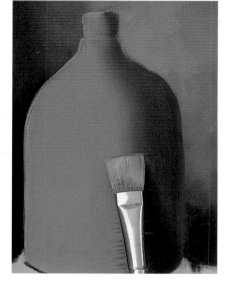

🌰 **STEP 4.** Finally, with a big, dry, soft brush, run down along the wiggled edge to smooth the wiggles out. This will take some practice but, as you can see, it's a valuable trick.

Painting Large Areas

The backgrounds of pictures are all important. We run into them in portraits (backgrounds), landscapes (skies) and still lifes (walls and drapery).

A basic rule for doing large areas is to do them in two stages: first, lay in the paint in the tones you want; second, work into this paint with some brushwork to move the paint into the effect you want.

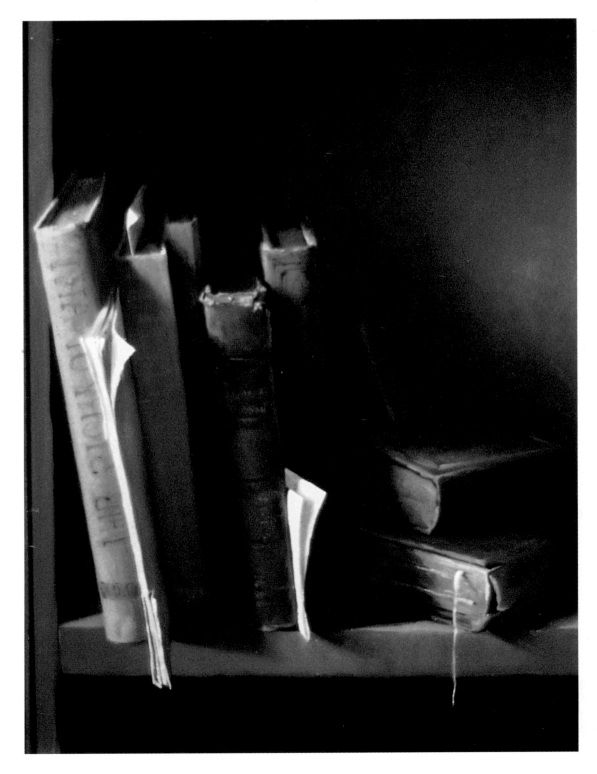

**A Good Read,
16 x 20",
*Private Collection.***
The drama of this picture is the *trompe l'loeil* quality. The books seem to extend beyond the picture plane, making it successful as a "fool-the-eye" composition. Dramatic, too, is the expanse of the background.

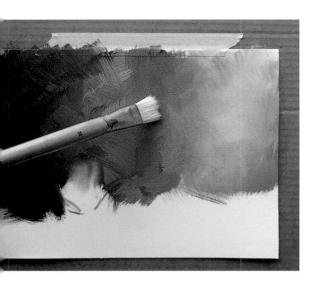

🍂 STEP 1. To begin your background, lay in the values very roughly, as seen here. Don't scrimp on the paint.

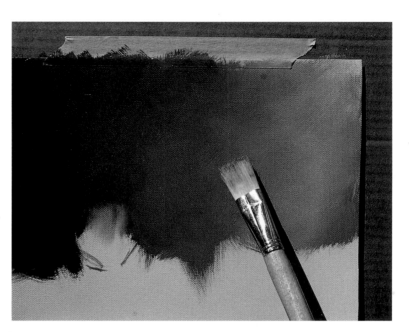

🍂 STEP 2. Next, with a large brush begin to smooth the tones together. Blend by using short "flipflop" strokes with your dry, clean brush, a large white bristle flat whose longer bristles are very handy for this kind of a job in painting. *IMPORTANT:* No matter what brush you use, it should be dry and clean.

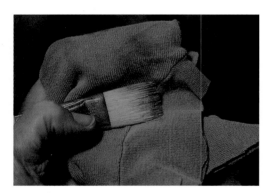

🍂 STEP 3. Constantly keep cleaning your brush by rubbing it against a Turkish towel rag. Don't clean with turpentine!

🍂 STEP 4. Now, with less pressure, smooth out some more, using the same white bristle flat.

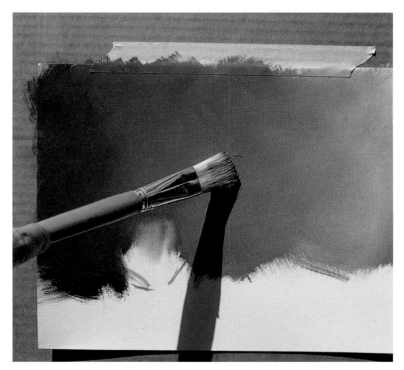

A Picture is Painted in Layers

If you could dissect a Rembrandt painting by stripping it off layer by layer, you'd find that the Old Master's thinking would be unbared. Surely, the lovely effects we find in paintings aren't a matter of one superficial layer. Instead, they're a result of many layers, each one doing its job well.

Here's a statue in front of a draped background. The steps that follow will show the development of the various stages of the painting.

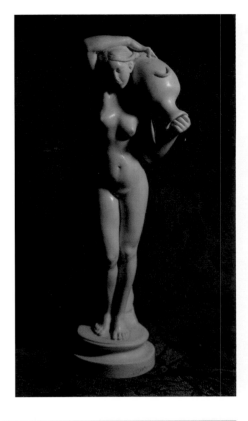

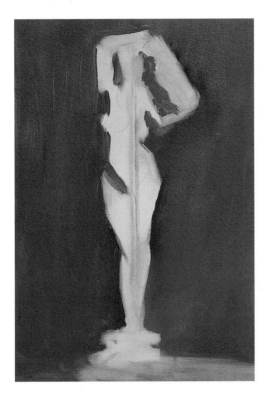

🍂 STEP 1. *The first stage.* The beginning of the form.

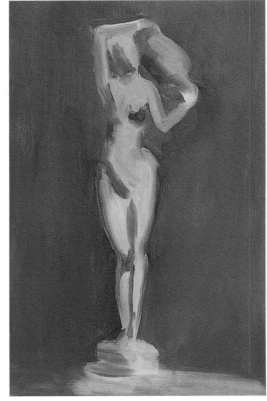

🍂 STEP 2. The form in a rough stage, done by working with the light side, the shadow and the background. *REMEMBER* — at this stage the basic shapes of light and dark should be your only concern. *No Details! No Blending.* Do one thing at a time. This layer serves to record the statue's shape and action. I grant you, it's hard to search out the beginning of any complete problem. But in paint, structure always comes first.

STEP 3. Now take a closer look at your subject matter. Redo the arm, and shape the bottom of the arm with the shadow.

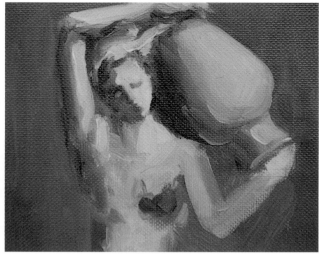

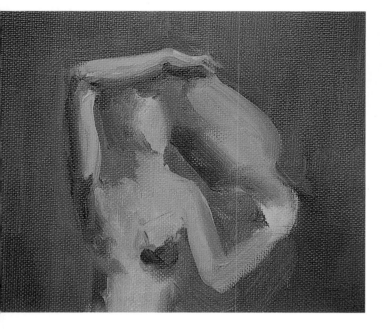

STEP 4. Redo the light side of the vase, head and arms, correcting them with shadows.

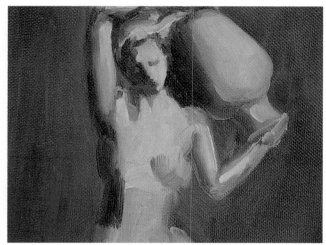

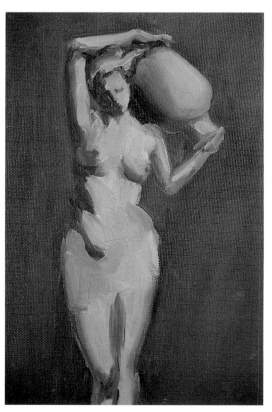

STEP 5. Redo the light side of the chest and breasts.

STEP 6. Shape the breasts with the shadows, and cut in the lower chest up to the breast shadows.

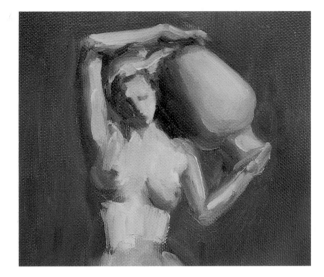

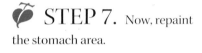 **STEP 7.** Now, repaint the stomach area.

A still life painter has to be a collector of various objects: pots, vases, baskets, porcelains, trays and also sculpture of every description. Statues of human figures and animals will also do much to further your study of those subjects.

STEP 8. *Finishing the painting.* This shows the second stage of development, a refinement of stage one. By this closer inspection, the basic structure is developed. The figure was again observed from the top down, and the highlights were added to finalize the modeling. The dimension was further developed by some darker accentuation to the shadow pattern.

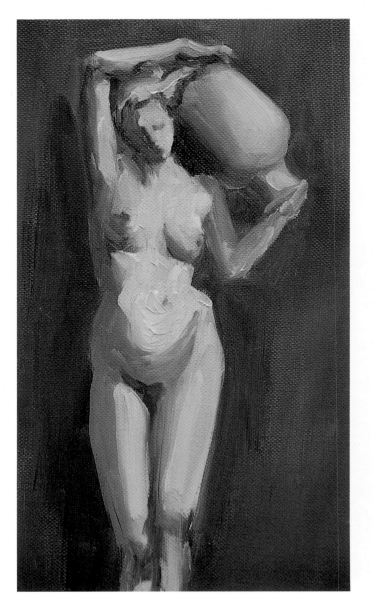

An Easy Procedure

Almost anything can be painted by massing in the correct silhouette and then adding lights and darks. I have found this procedure particularly helpful when painting flowers, especially roses.

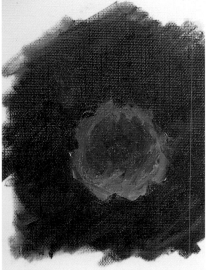 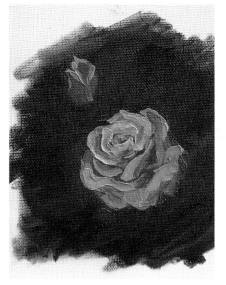 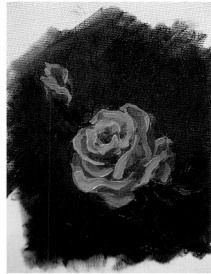

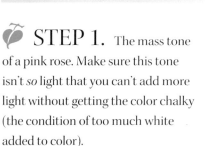 **STEP 1.** The mass tone of a pink rose. Make sure this tone isn't *so* light that you can't add more light without getting the color chalky (the condition of too much white added to color).

STEP 2. The light areas have been added.

STEP 3. The darks have been added. When painting flowers — or anything, for that matter — it's far easier to add the lights to the mass tone first, then accent with the darks.

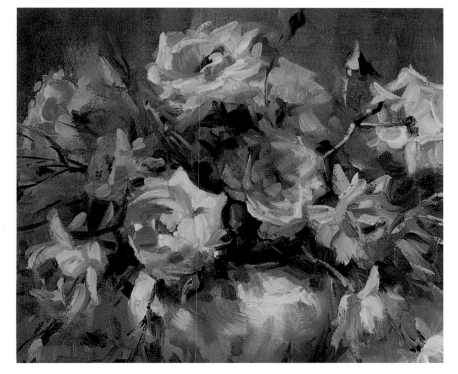

In this detail of a painting of roses, we see the procedure in actual practice.

The Significance of Found-and-Lost Line

An important ingredient in doing a representational painting is the aspect of dimension. We are ever conscious (or should be) of the two-dimensional surface on which we intend to plant our three-dimensional interpretation of our inspiration. And, believe me, any device we can utilize to pull this caper off is most welcome indeed. The five tone values, which you can refer to on page 104, are a major aid to the painter in his bid to inject dimension to the aforementioned two-dimensional surface.

Another critical element is a technique which, I have found, is not generally heralded in painting instruction books. It is "found-and-lost line," a term I use to describe the treatment of any subject's outline. I admit that it's a misnomer because, in painting, there are no lines; they are edges that abut each other thus creating "lines." In painting, you might say that drawing is more a matter of making sharp and fuzzy edges and not a matter of making lines. I have used this term, though, for half a century; I'm used to it; it works for me.

Found-and-lost line describes sharply defined edges (found) and fuzzy, soft edges (lost). It's highly important because it deals with the shape of things and is essential in the crystallization of the realism of three dimensions.

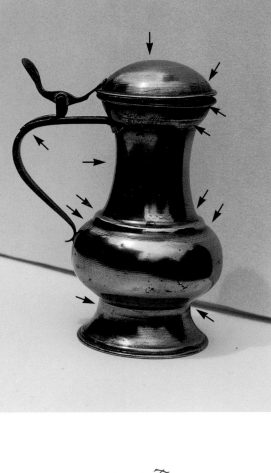

STEP 1. I have used this pewter tankard in a great many still life compositions. I like its shape and the pewter texture suggests a certain type of theme to a painting. In this photograph of the tankard, I have used arrows to point out all of the places where the edge is lost.

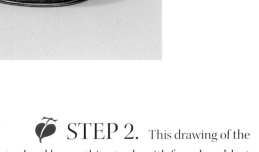

STEP 2. This drawing of the tankard has nothing to do with found-and-lost line. It's merely the construction of the object.

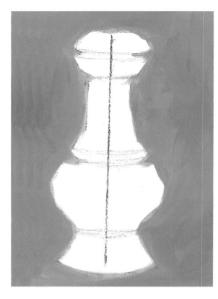

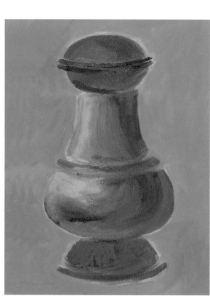

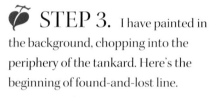

✿ **STEP 4.** The background tone has been made to fall into the object to show its structure. This was done by pulling up on the pressure of the brush as it cuts the object's shape out into the wet background. The sharp and fuzzy edges (found and lost) show up on this interpretation of the tankard; compare this step to the photograph that contains the arrows at all lost edges.

✿ **STEP 3.** I have painted in the background, chopping into the periphery of the tankard. Here's the beginning of found-and-lost line.

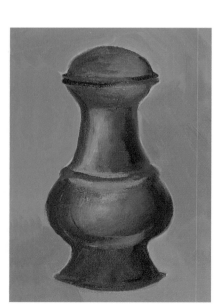

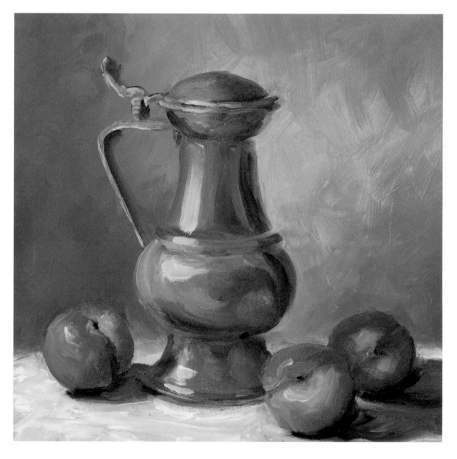

✿ **STEP 5.** In this diagram, I have sharpened the entire outline of the tankard to show you how flat the object looks without any lost or fuzzy edges.

To sum up: Where do found-and-lost lines appear? Wherever a shape turns in a different direction. In portraiture, for instance, where the top of the head meets the side of the head, the point where they meet is a found line. On the other hand, the top and down planes are lost lines. On a tree trunk, the found line is where the light strikes; the shadow side would be the lost line.

How to Observe Carefully

Since a dimensional effect is a realistic effect, your observation should be coupled with your awareness of the whole depth or solidity of the subject. I have found an easy way to explain this more clearly by asking you to visualize a sliced loaf of bread standing on end. Observe it from the top down, one slice at a time. I see everything in this world as a sliced loaf of bread, and I paint one slice at a time. Here's how, in my portrait of Michael.

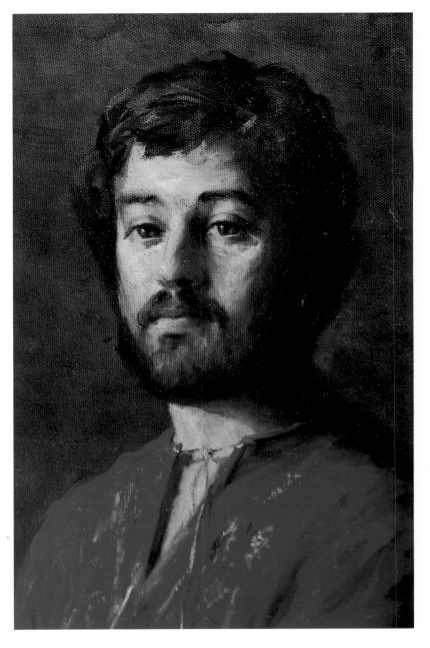

Michael as Othello, 20 x 24"
Since Michael Sachnoff, an old friend, was an opera buff, I chose to paint him as a slightly lighter-skinned Othello, the tragic Moor of Verdi's opera. For this lesson, I have isolated the eye area to demonstrate how I saw him as a loaf of bread.

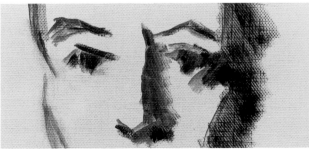

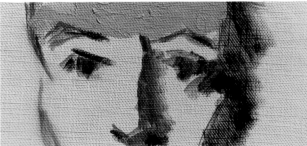

🍂 SKETCH. In this sketch, we're looking at the eye area of the face, and are now ready to begin, painting one slice at a time.

🍂 SLICE 1. The forehead. The flesh tone, incidentally, could be any warm color into white.

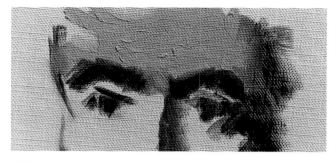

❦ SLICE 2. The top of the eyebrows meeting the forehead.

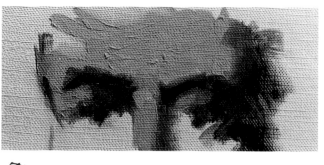

❦ SLICE 3. The bottom of the eyebrows.

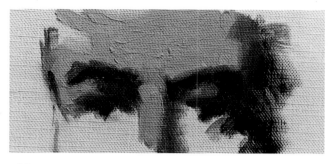

❦ SLICE 4. The shadow, caused by the lid, on the upper eye area.

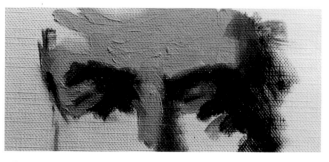

❦ SLICE 5. The upper lid.

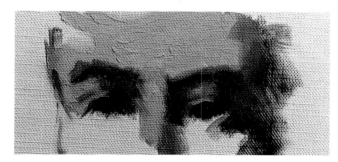

❦ SLICE 6. The shadow on the eyeball caused by the upper lid and also the iris of the eye.

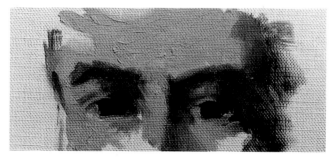

❦ SLICE 7. The white of one eye and the upper part of the lower lid.

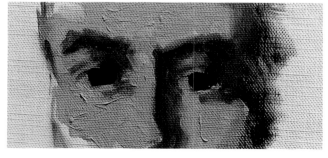

❦ SLICE 8. The shadow on the lower lid.

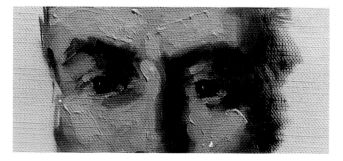

❦ SLICE 9. Now the lighter lights and darker darks accentuate the form.

Highlights

Highlights appear on the concave and convex planes that are toward the light. They should never be thought of as little white spots. They're important tone values that you use to show the fullness and solidity of an object. Highlights are the last tones you apply in your painting. Sometimes highlights are sharp and sometimes they're very diffused. The seemingly colorless spot that is a highlight is not colorless at all; it is actually a very light colored spot. A highlight is *always* the complementary color to the color it's on (aside from brass and copper, the only exceptions to the rule). Therefore, on a red apple the highlight is white with just a speck of green. Refer to the *The Color Recipes* (Section II) to find the highlight color of the various subjects.

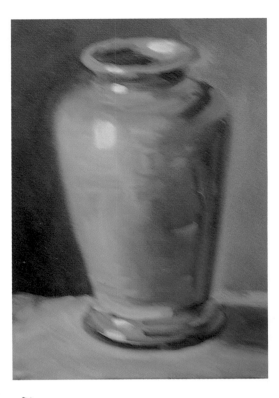

STEP 1. Apply the highlight.

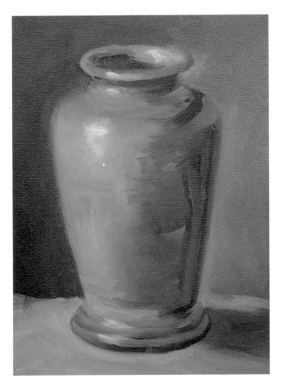

STEP 2. Fuse it into the mass tone.

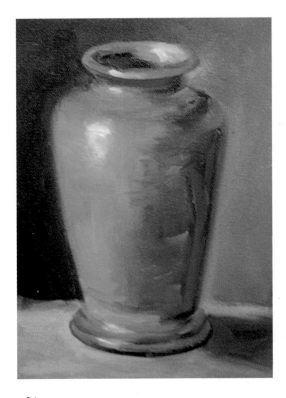

STEP 3. Now reapply the highlight. Notice how each one shows the form that swoops out toward the light or swoops back from the light.

Achieving Textures

I have never had an exhibition of my paintings without at least one person saying, "I would love to paint like you." Then, "Do you have room in your classes for one more?" My classes have been popular over the years because students *do* want to paint like I do, which is in an extremely traditional style.

The element that makes my paintings so popular with students — and many other people, I am pleased to say — is the manner in which I choose to interpret the world around me. I agree with the critics of representational painting that a camera does do a more *accurate* job of recording this world, but *my* interpretation is personal to me and nothing can duplicate the intimate experience that I undergo in my quest to capture it all successfully on canvas. An important part of the story that I want to tell with paint is the attention to the textures of things. And all things have textures.

For the portrait painter, it's the excitement of the model's complexion: the smoothness of young skin, the character lines of the aged; the different types of hair; getting the look of young lips and the lips of an older person; young eyes and old eyes; and, overall, the challenge of portraying human beings on canvas as I see them.

For the still life painter, the joy of painting the skin of an apple, the blossoms of flowers, the shine of metals, the transparency of glass, and the luster of satin, to name a few.

Outdoor painters don't encounter the complicated textures that portrait and still life painters must contend with. The paint application that's used outdoors mainly shows direction, flat like the ground or slanted like a roof top. The landscapist's texture is light that just happens to be striking the composition. While portrait and still life painters also paint the effect of light, in their case, it records subjects that are in closer focus.

It's fitting that the last section of this book is all about textures, because, in many paintings, textures are the very last things the artist adds.

Why Textures Appear

All textures can be interpreted with paint. Making velvet look like it has a pile and brass look like it shines is a challenge. It's impossible to record them if two very important factors of the painting process aren't employed:

TONE VALUE. The painter must respect and be aware of contrasts of tone value that are caused by light.

RHYTHM AND ORDER OF APPLICATION. The painter must realize that the paint can be applied in layers, each one satisfying a facet of the texture's profoundness. Paint can be applied in different directions and in various thicknesses.

Before we get into studying textures, let's first explore and understand the principles of *tone value*. If you grasp its importance in obtaining texture, all textures — even those not covered in these pages — will be easy for you to paint.

Look at the two illustrations. The drape on the left is wool; the one on the right is satin. They're both the same value. Notice how the same lighting on these two different textures reveals each one's distinct texture. Surely, you can see that if you record these contrasts correctly you'll paint each texture accurately.

The painter must respect and be aware of contrasts of tone value that are caused by light.

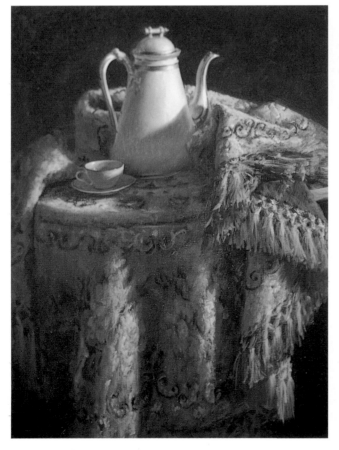

ILLUSTRATION 1.

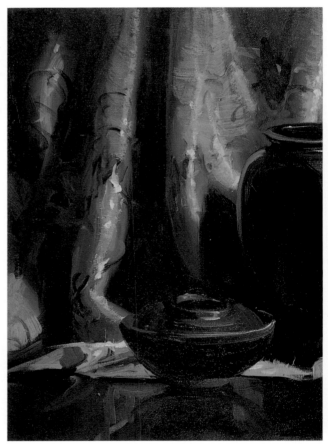

ILLUSTRATION 2.

Light's Paint Translation

Light makes us see as we do, it causes color to appear, and because it travels in a straight line, light causes contrasts. Planes that aren't turned toward the light are shaded or darker. It's imperative, then, to have one source of light since it causes five distinct tone values:

1. **Body Tone**
2. **Body Shadow**
3. **Cast Shadow**
4. **Reflection**
5. **Highlight**

Paint has three different properties:

1. It can be many different *tones*.
2. It comes in all *colors*.
3. It has *substance*.

Since light causes color and tone, paint must be thought of as the physical substitute for light. Paint does to the canvas what light does to the subject. Paint can do everything that lighting shows up. But paint can never be brass or apples; it can only record how brass and apples appear.

Many students are overly concerned with color instead of with tone. Color has three properties: *Hue, Intensity and Tone.* Tone, by far, is the most important of the three. You can recognize the texture of anything in black and white. When you watch a black-and-white television set, you may miss the color, but you don't need it to see the picture and to comprehend everything about it. Virtually everything is recognizable regardless of the color that's not being shown.

This painting of a silver coffee pot illustrates how one source of light dramatically shows up an object's dimension. Actually, using one source of light is simulating a universal truth: the sun that lights the outdoors. To point out how important this one source of light is, a white statue would barely be visible if it were illuminated on all its sides.

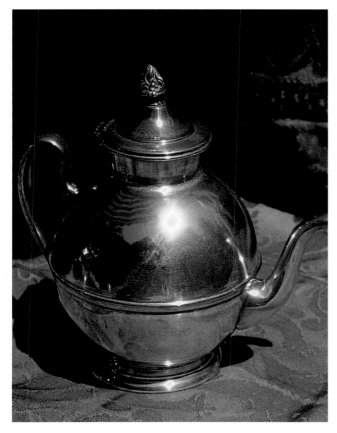

ILLUSTRATION 1.

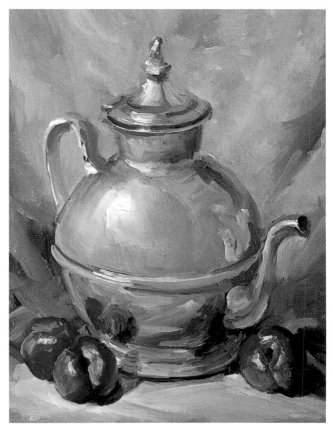

ILLUSTRATION 2.

The Five Tone Values

Let's now look at the silver coffee pot and strip it down into the individual elements of the tone values:

1. **BODY TONE.** The value of an object in relation to its background.

2. **BODY SHADOW.** A darkening of the tone of the object where its shape turns away from the source of light.

3. **CAST SHADOW.** Darker tones on areas that are shadowed because something is in the way of the light.

4. **HIGHLIGHT.** The lightest tone on an object, and it's where the light strikes it directly. Highlights are on concave and convex planes that are in direct line with the light.

5. **REFLECTIONS.** Tones caused by surrounding areas or objects (these are never lighter than the body tone).

Each tone value plays its part in recording the object's texture. If one is to be considered the most important, it would be the highlight because the characteristic of the highlight dictates the texture most dramatically. The most common mistake is to want to put a highlight on and find it doesn't show up because the object was massed in too light in the beginning. And when painting white objects, make sure the mass tone is darker than white to leave you a tone for the highlight.

 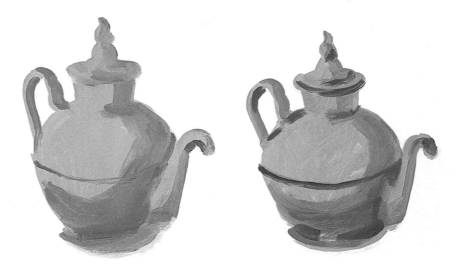

BODY TONE.   **BODY SHADOW.**   **CAST SHADOWS.**

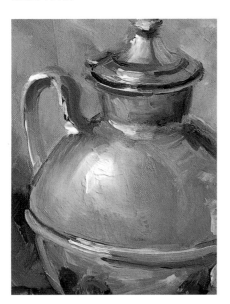

The most common mistake is to want to put a highlight on and find it doesn't show up because the object was massed in too light in the beginning.

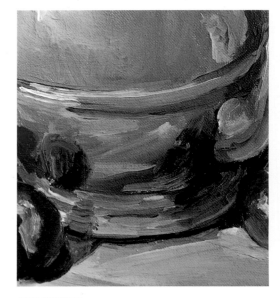

HIGHLIGHT.   **REFLECTIONS.**

The Two Basic Textures

Now that we realize that an object's texture is mostly a matter of tone, we have to consider how these tones can be applied. Basically, there are two types of textures — *reflecting and non-reflecting (shiny and dull).*

1. **REFLECTING OBJECTS ARE ANYTHING THAT SHINE.** Glass is the most reflecting, silver is another, as are all metals, waxed wood, satin, hair and anything that's wet.

2. **NON-REFLECTING OBJECTS ARE THOSE THAT DON'T SHINE OR HAVE A MATTE SURFACE.** A clay pot and slate are the most non-reflecting surfaces. Stone crocks, most fruits, baskets, linen and skin are some other non-reflecting objects.

It's important to classify things this way because it's the key to getting their textures. Another factor to be aware of, is when painting reflecting and non-reflecting textures, you must start them differently, as follows:

Non-reflecting objects are massed in right from the start in two values: *Body Tone* and *Body Shadow*. You can see this in the painting of the wooden bucket along with a sketch that illustrates this principle.

Reflecting objects are massed in *entirely in their Body Tone* in contrast to the background, as illustrated in the painting of the glass bottle and fruit.

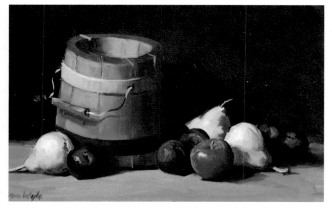

NON-REFLECTING OBJECT A.

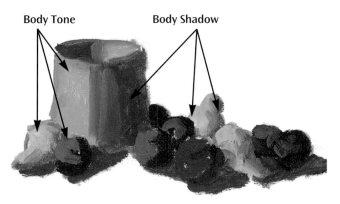

NON-REFLECTING OBJECT B. Non-reflecting objects are massed in right from the start in two values.

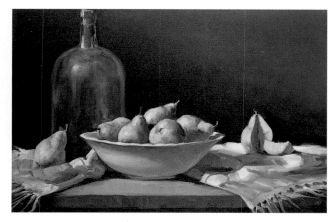

REFLECTING OBJECT A.

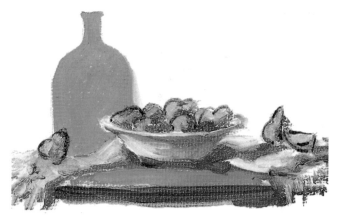

REFLECTING OBJECT B. Reflecting objects are massed in entirely in one tone value.

Don't Let Textures Fool You!

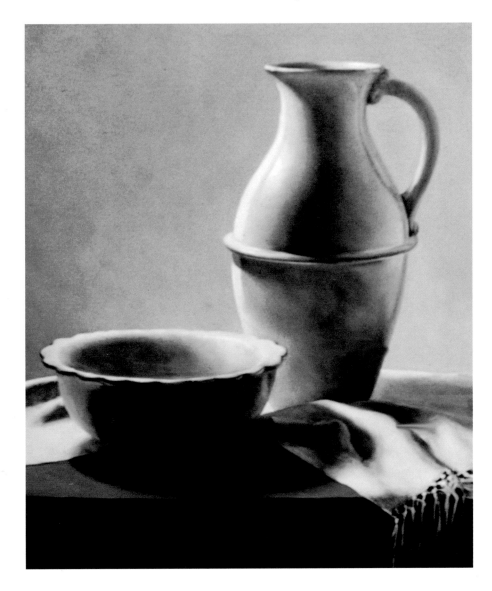

Many things that are non-reflecting can get reflections. A good example is this ceramic pitcher *(left)*, which is basically a non-reflecting object. But it has just enough of a glaze (a *ceramic* glaze, that is) to enable it to pick up reflections. Notice, though, that these reflections still don't interrupt the object's basic *light and dark sides.*

A reflecting object, like the pewter tray *(below)*, is shown in a condition where its reflecting nature doesn't show. The tones arrange themselves much like a non-reflecting object. As you see, it can have a strong light-and-dark pattern, which disguises its reflecting quality.

The first step in painting a texture is seeing the texture in a good light and analyzing it. Then translate what you see in terms of paint, making your very first application record the essence of texture.

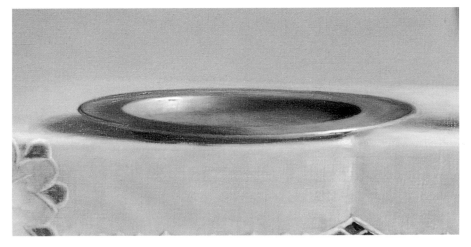

The first step in painting a texture is seeing the texture in a good light and analyzing it.

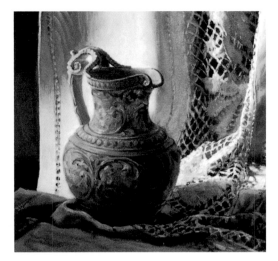

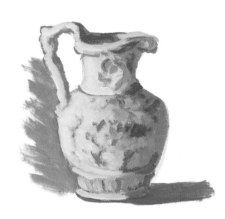

TEXTURES 1. The sculptured pitcher is definitely non-reflecting and has to be started with two values. All objects that have an inner shape that differs from its out-line must be considered non-reflecting. The shape of the shadow shows the shape of the inner drawing.

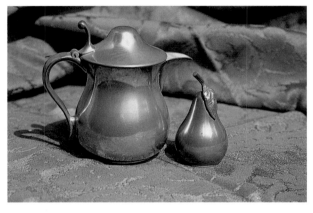

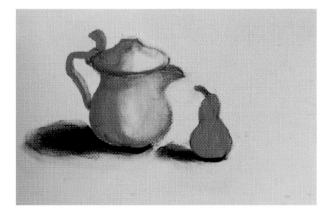

TEXTURES 2. The two metal objects are reflecting and could be started with two tones or massed in with one. The illustration on the right shows how you can start to paint reflecting objects in either of two ways. Some objects in certain lighting are a toss-up; dark objects are always massed in with one tone.

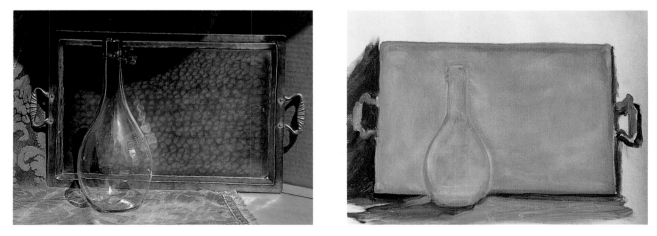

TEXTURES 3. Silver and glass are definitely reflecting surfaces and can be started with one mass tone. All objects classified as reflecting have sharp highlights that are in great contrast to the mass tone. That's what causes a shine.

You Need a Brush for Every Job

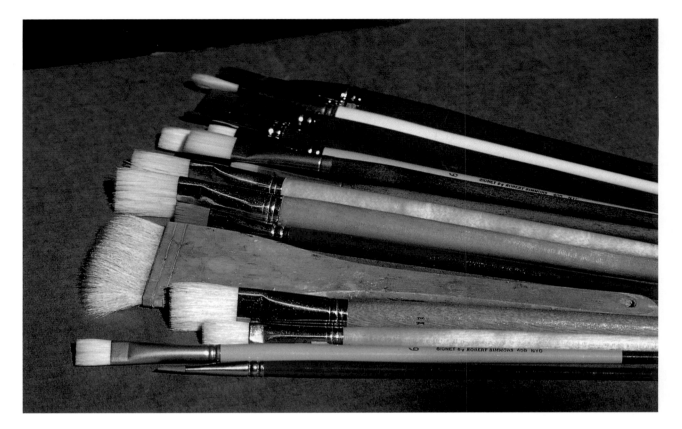

In order to make a paint application marry a texture, you have to describe in words the feeling of the texture so you can find the brush or painting knife that will carry out your orders. We do, after all, want to use the tool that will make the job as easy as possible. For instance, if you want a painted area smooth, you need a "smoother" (a large, soft brush); if you want to make little lines, you need a "little line maker" (a small round red sable brush). Just as you can't do fine cabinetwork with a ripsaw, you can't get an effect with paint without the right brushes. Since there are so many different textures, it seems logical that you'd need a wide variety of brushes to open the "texture door" for you. Here are the ones I have and what I use them for:

1. **LARGE RED SABLE FAN BLENDER** (size 6) to smooth and blend areas.

2. **LARGE JAPANESE HAKE BRUSH** to smooth in large areas or dust away harshness.

3. **LARGE WHITE BRISTLE FLAT** (size 10 or 12) to drag over an area to impart a tooth or feeling of thickness.

4. **SET OF RED SABLE BRIGHTS** (sizes 3 to 20) for general painting.

5. **SET OF WHITE BRISTLE FILBERTS** (sizes 3 to 12) for rougher general painting.

6. **SET OF WHITE BRISTLE FLATS** (sizes 4 to 9) to start the picture.

7. **SET OF RED SABLE ROUNDS** (sizes 2 to 6) for final fussy textures, such as patterns, highlights, stripes, etc.

Brush Manipulation

Along with *progression of application*, there's the factor of *manipulation*.

Progression is applying layers of paint one on top of the other, each satisfying a facet of the object's texture.

Manipulation is just moving an application with a second brush action. For example, in order to blend two values in a portrait, first apply the paint to record the tones and then move the tones into a textural effect. You know you can only do one thing at a time, so first recreate the model's shape and form; then record his texture or skin.

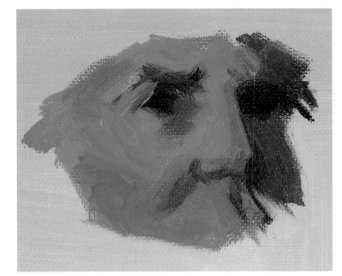

1. Initial lay in of paint (first part of progression).

2. Manipulation of the initial application of paint.

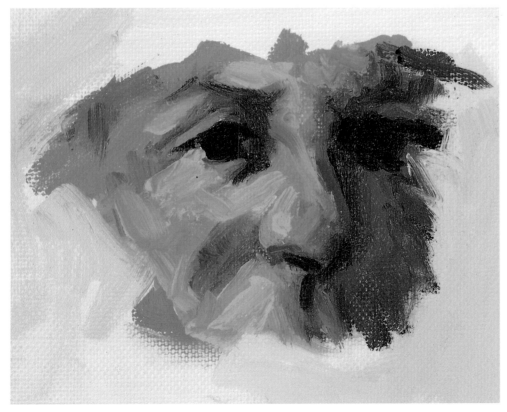

3. The detail of the finished painting.

Texture by Darker Applications

A painting is put together with thoughts and each thought is a layer of paint. In relation to this philosophy, the late Thomas Hart Benton said: "I'd like to be rich enough to buy a Titian so I could strip it away layer by layer to see how that old master thought."

As you've already seen, progression of application is a vital ingredient in the painting process. Let's now put it to work to paint the texture of old wood. We see the grain, the slats, the wall, but we can't make the wall by painting the grain. That would be just like trying to make a forest by painting leaves.

It's essential to find the beginning. Say to yourself: "I'm going to paint a wall that's made of slats that are grained." Whenever a subject has a pattern such as grain in wood and marble or prints in fabrics, it's best to lay in a basic tone of paint and then, after the basic tone has dried, add the pattern in a second application.

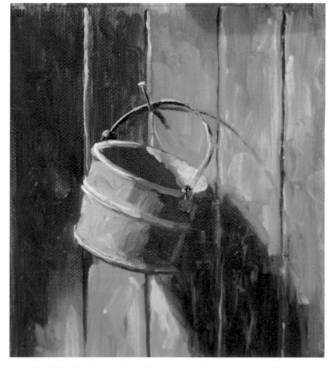

Detail of finished painting, featuring old wood as a background.

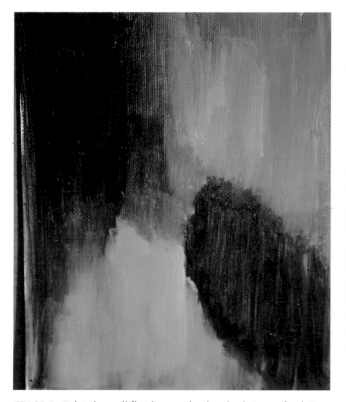

STAGE 1. Paint the wall first by massing in a basic tone of paint.

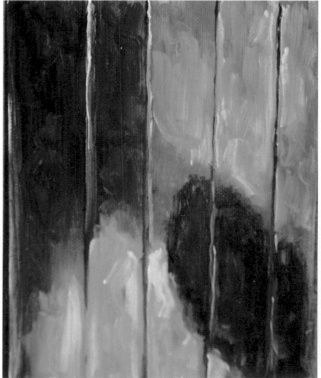

STAGE 2. Paint the slats next by adding their pattern with lights and darks.

Getting Texture With Glazes

There are two ways to add characteristics to a dried, painted surface: one is *glazing*, the other is *scumbling*. Adding wood grain is a glazing operation. You should glaze whenever you've decided that the pattern, or the character added, is a darker value. It should be embedded in the surface. It should not become a new dimension. Other textures that should be glazed are the blue pattern on Delft, decorations on any porcelain, or prints, plaids and stripes on fabrics.

The application that adds the decorative characteristic should be thin so it doesn't stand apart from the first layer. Make a "glazing medium" of half linseed oil and half turpentine and thin your paint with it. Don't ever use any white when adding your textures because a glaze is thinned paint that's transparent. White, as you know, will make any mixture opaque, and an opaque application would cover the basic tone rather than imparting the grain or pattern to it. Adding the grain is done in two stages:

You should glaze whenever you've decided that the pattern is a darker value.

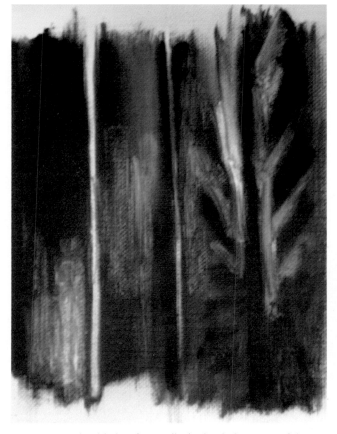

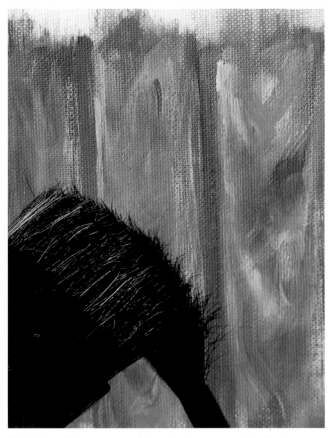

STAGE 1. On the dried surface, strike in the darker tones of the grain darker than you see them.

STAGE 2. With a rag or a soft brush, wipe some of the dark tones away in the direction of the wood grain. (The brush used here is a Japanese Hake.)

Texturing by Lighter Applications

When textures stand out from the surface — such as anything rough — they have to be recorded by adding lighter toned applications. A lighter application will almost always have white in it, making it opaque. This kind of application is called *scumbling*.

Let's fit this term into normal conversation to see how a form of scumbling was used to create the linen that's portrayed in my painting of "Cutwork Cloth," shown on this page.

First, in *Figure 1*, a general tone was used to mass in the front plane where the linen hangs down. In *Figure 2*, lighter tones were worked in to suggest slight ripples.

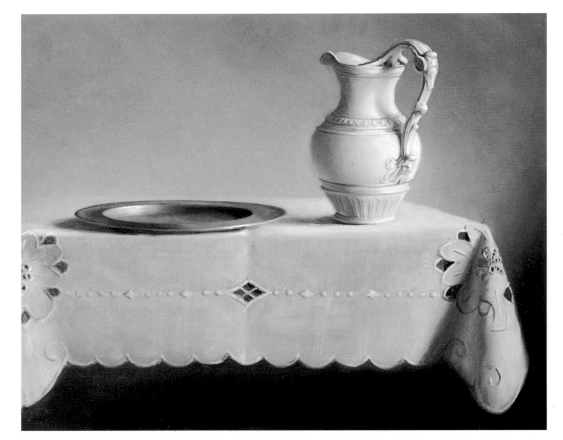

**Cutwork Cloth,
20 x 24",
oil on canvas,
Private collection.**
The beauty of the elegantly embroidered cloth is brought out so dramatically in this painting.

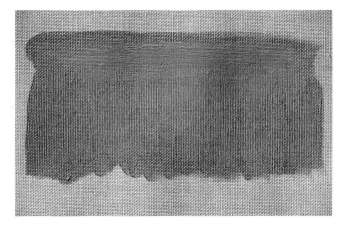

FIGURE 1.

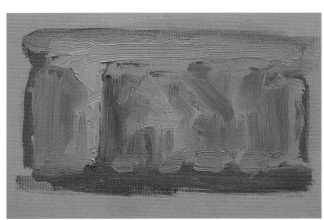

FIGURE 2.

Getting Texture With Scumbles

The area had to be dry to the touch before the subtle linen texture was applied. To show the delicate weave of the linen cloth, a light value was dragged over the dried area in, first, vertical strokes *(Figure 3)* and, then, horizontal strokes *(Figure 4)*. The brush was fairly dry — excess paint being wiped away on a cloth. This is important, because this kind of scumbling isn't covering the surface, it is just grazing over the surface in spots. (The brush shown here is a large bristle cutter, a sign painter's instrument. A large white bristle flat would do as well.)

The embroidery was added last. First, it was planned out in a lighter value with paint that was quite thinned with medium to make it flow more easily *(Figure 5)*. Then, when those areas were completely dry, the lights and darks were added with thicker paint *(Figure 6)*. The texture of the embroidery was stroked with the brush in the same way that the actual embroidery was sewn with needle and thread.

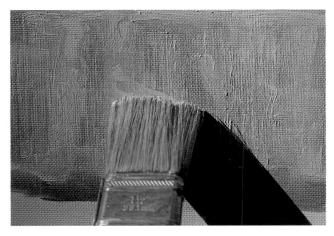

FIGURE 3.

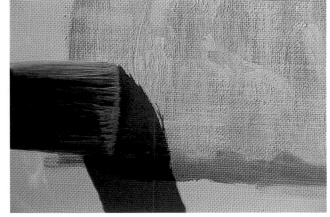

FIGURE 4.

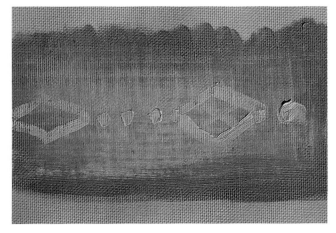

FIGURE 5.

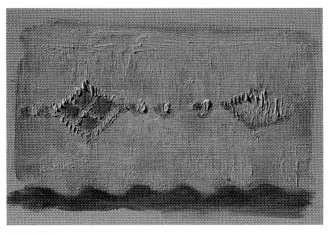

FIGURE 6.

Understanding Glazing & Scumbling

Developing a painting to the degree that the viewer says: "It looks so real, I can reach out and touch it," can never be done in one application. That look is a matter of refinement, which glazing and scumbling can give to an already painted area. Since they are so important to achieving textures, I must carefully define glazing and scumbling because they are the ways of applying subsequent layers of paint.

Glazing

• Glazing is an application of transparent color.

• A glaze can only be applied to a dry area.

• A glaze never covers the area but only adds color to it.

Many students think a glaze is a *medium*. Wrong! A glaze is paint that's often *thinned* with a medium. The most important point about a glaze is that it's an application of paint with no white in it. The addition of white makes any color opaque and a glaze must be transparent. Here's a list of what glazes can and can't do and when to use a glaze:

1. A glaze never adds texture. It only adds color and improves an existing texture.

2. A glaze *always darkens* an area.

3. A dark glaze of color over a light area gives a luminous look to the area.

4. Whole objects or only portions of objects can be glazed. If you've painted an apple and the color doesn't look lush enough, make it a lush red by glazing a mixture of Grumbacher Red and Alizarin Crimson over the entire apple. On the other hand, on a yellow apple that has a reddish, more ripened spot, paint the apple all yellow and when it's dry, glaze the red on.

5. Glazing never adds dimension. It becomes part of the dimension it's painted on. A glaze of Burnt Sienna over an already painted copper pot will be dark where it goes over the darker areas and light where it goes over the lighter areas.

6. Use glazes whenever you want to richen a color.

7. Remember, a glaze is always applied over a painted area. You can't glaze a bare canvas.

8. The notes on the music *(pages 115 & 122)* were glazed on with a mixture of Ivory Black and Burnt Umber and thinned with a medium. An opaque mixture would have made the notes stand out too much, while glazing them on made them part of the music.

7. Any gold decoration can be glazed on with Raw Sienna and then a highlight must be added. You can always work opaque passages into a glaze *(refer to Section I, My Basic Palette, how to paint a gilt-edged book with Raw Sienna)*.

Because glazing darkens an area, it enables you to add more lights again. Once you realize how important this is, you'll appreciate how invaluable glazing is.

Scumbling

Think of scumbling as glazing's opposite.

• A scumble is always opaque (has a degree of white),

• A scumble is always used to *lighten* an area.

• A scumble is used to fuse or gray the area.

Use scumbling to add the fuzz to peaches, the waxiness to apples, the mist over the docks, the silvery look to the ocean, the pile on velvet, the shine on wood, and many other similar textures. There are two ways to apply a scumble:

1. You can rub it on

2. You can drag it on.

And, of course, a scumble must always be added to a dry surface.

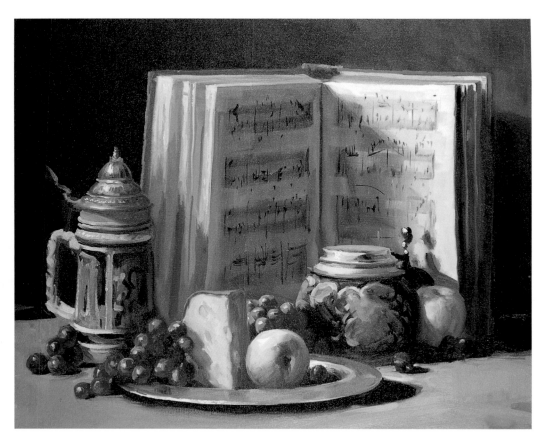

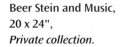

Beer Stein and Music, 20 x 24", *Private collection.*
A good example of one of the reasons to use a glaze is the addition of musical notes, which then look like they are part of the page rather than dark values that were just plopped on with heavier paint.

An example of a glaze.

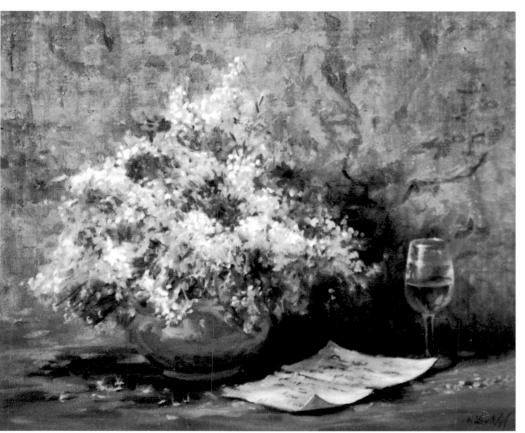

The Love Letter, 22 x 28", *Private collection.*
Whenever I received a letter, especially from Herb during our courtship years, I would pour a glass of wine and settle in to read and, invariably, savor it. This picture was painted in memory of those moments. The tapestry in the background was scumbled to achieve the effect.

An example of a scumble.

Put Textures on Stage

Another way to achieve textures is to make sure you mass in the pattern of the light areas in a tone that's darker than you see it. This will make it possible for you to add the feeling of the texture by adding lighter passages. It's essential to do this because to record a texture, you have to be extremely convincing due to the limits of the two-dimensional surface. The texture of an object, after all, is not only something to look at, but is thought of as something that we can hold and feel. To convince the viewer of this, you must accentuate the look of the texture.

When I painted the strawberry baskets, I had to make sure that the thin wooden slats, which are so characteristic of this type of container, were recognized as such by the viewer. By putting the light value in darker than it is *(Figure 1)* and adding lighter lights, I painted what the wood is about instead of just the way it looks, making my paint presentation very convincing *(Figure 2)*. The lighter tones were added with a palette knife, a great tool for

getting textural looks. I used the palette knife to add tone to an already massed in area. If I had used it directly, it would just have given me thick paint.

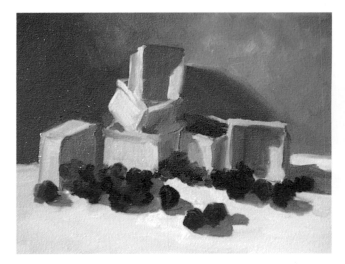

FIGURE 1. Laying in the masses in a darker tone, left me room to lighten greatly.

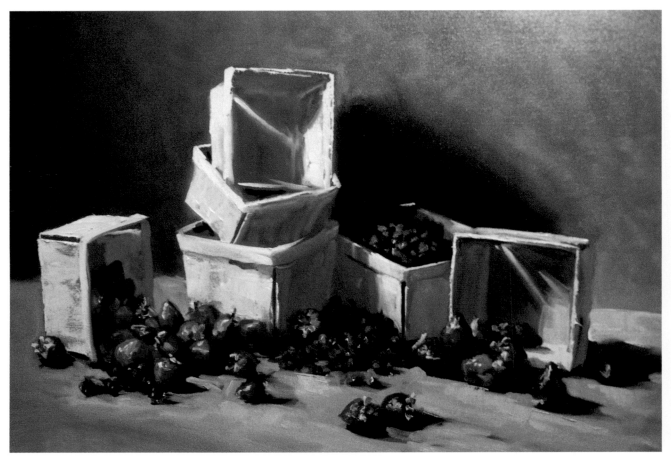

FIGURE 2. Strawberry Baskets, 18 x 24".
The thin, wooden slats were all important to the identity of the baskets.

Give Your Paint a Chance to Show the Texture

What could be different as subject matter than a torn sheet of music and an ocean wave? They are surely worlds apart as subject matter and, yet, they are painted in precisely the same manner by massing in the light areas darker than they actually are.

Sheet Music

1. A photograph of the music.
2. The paper is massed in with a value that's darker than it is. Once the lighter lights and darker darks have been added, the notes will be painted in last.

Ocean Waves

1. It's easier to add lighter lights to light areas than adding darker tones to light areas.
2. Compare this with the finished painting. You will see how much lighter I was able to go.

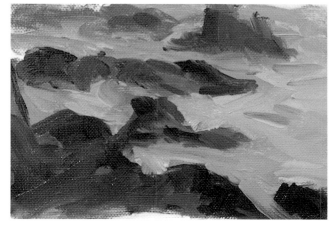

OCEAN WAVES 1.

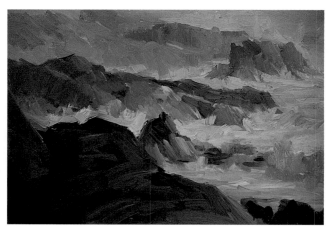

OCEAN WAVES 2.

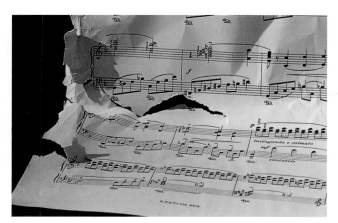

SHEET MUSIC 1.

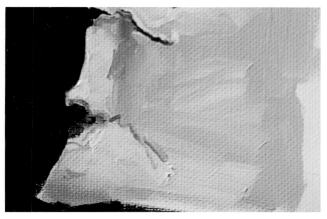

SHEET MUSIC 2.

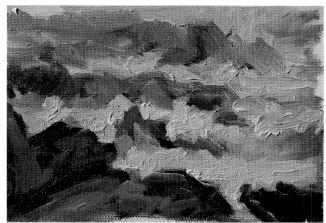

Bass Rocks, Gloucester, Mass., 16 x 20".

The finished painting. The student would have painted this picture by making the light areas too light and then trying to add the darks.

Understanding Drapery

1. Any drapery, whether it's satin, velvet, silk or linen, will unfold under your brush if your brush records the five tone values that light imposes upon the drapery. These tone values are: *Body Tone, Body Shadow, Cast Shadow, Highlight, Reflection.* Since these five values are the substance of your picture of drapery, you have to think of which one to set down first. Here are some helpful hints:

2. Any *dark-toned* material should be massed in with the overall dark tone to which the lighter tone can be added. Then, add the dark shadows.

3. Any *light-toned* material should be started by painting the dark shadow patterns first and then painting the light body tone.

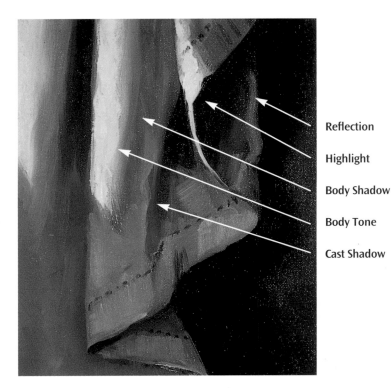

Reflection

Highlight

Body Shadow

Body Tone

Cast Shadow

DRAPERY 1.

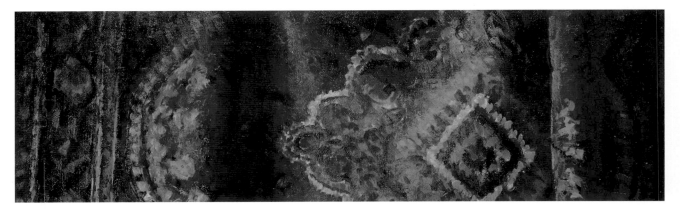

DRAPERY 2.

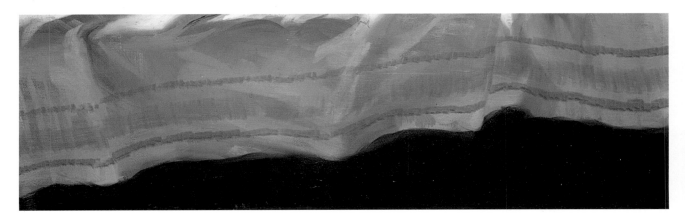

DRAPERY 3.

How to Paint Drapery

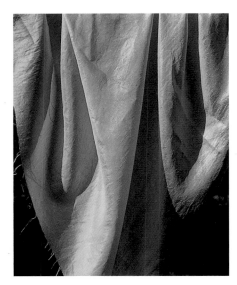

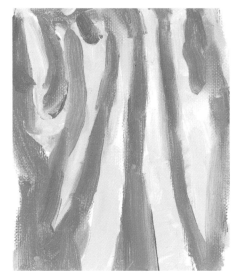

FIGURE 1 & 1A. On the left is a photo of the drape. The painting on the right is the start of the painting of the drape showing the mass tones of light and dark.

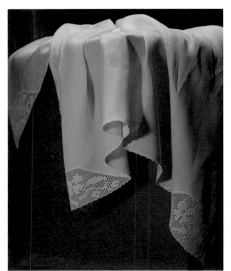

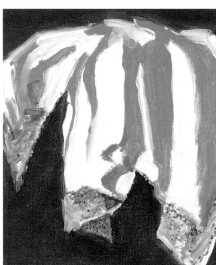

FIGURE 2 & 2A. On the left is a photo of a cutwork cloth drape. The painting on the right shows the rudimentary start to establish light and dark patterns.

To paint anything, it's absolutely essential to simplify what you see into masses of light values and dark values. Drapery is also a texture that's merely a matter of light and dark masses.

When painting most folds in any fabric, apply the paint in the direction that's opposite of the way the drape is falling. Then, if you're painting smooth fabric like satin, blend the paint in the direction of the fold. But you'll want to leave your strokes unblended when painting fabrics like velvet because of the pile that's so vital to the texture. In the diagram of a satin fold *(Figure 3)*, the area above the line shows the initial application of paint, done with teethlike strokes. The area below line shows the area smoothed out and blended in an opposite direction.

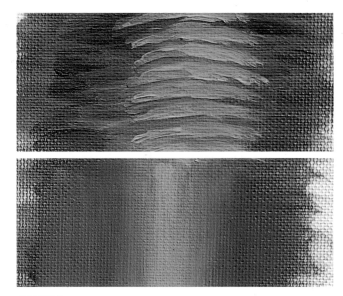

FIGURE 3.

Dramatizing Texture

1. At first glance, this texture and arrangement looks fearfully difficult But anything becomes possible and easy if we can find a simple beginning.

2. To begin, ask yourself this question: What tones am I going to make the background, sugar bowl and fabric? The answer will direct you to lay in the values of those areas with no regard to their texture or identity.

3. Now, with the addition of lighter lights and darker darks, these masses have been turned into these textures. Naturally, the fringe was put in last.

You can see that the painting is an interpretation of the subject. This is the personal touch that gives a painting originality.

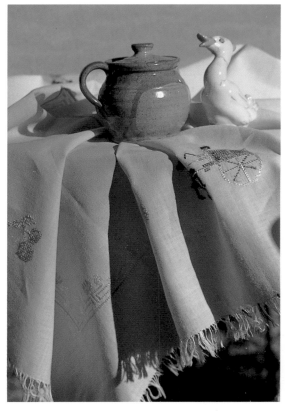

STAGE 1.

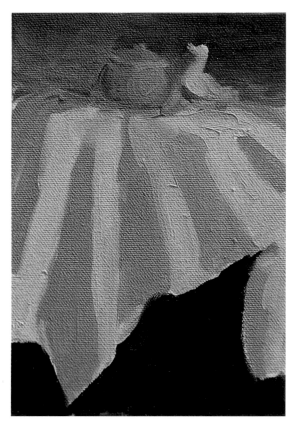

STAGE 2.

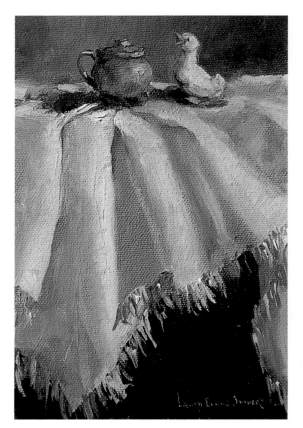

STAGE 3.

The Importance of the Highlight on Glass

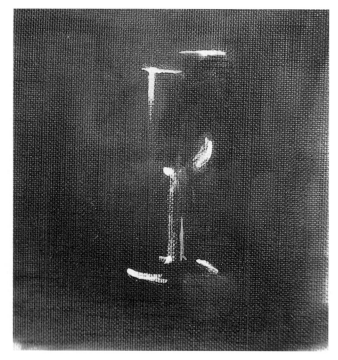

FIGURE 1.

The secret of painting glass is to realize how important the highlight is. It not only records the highly reflecting texture of glass but it also shows the shape of a glass object. In fact, you can paint the illusion of a glass object by only recording the highlights that strike the planes that are in direct line with the light, as seen in *Figure1*.

The transparency of glass is shown by painting on the back of the glass the very light colored tone that's caused by the light passing through the glass *(Figure 2)*.

These two tone values should be accentuated since they present the very nature of anything that's glasslike, such as the eye *(Figure 3)*.

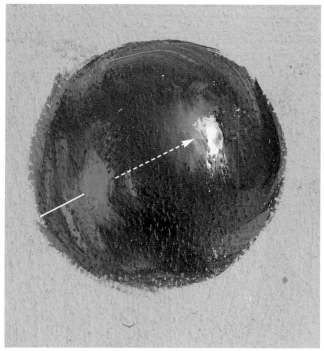

FIGURE 2.

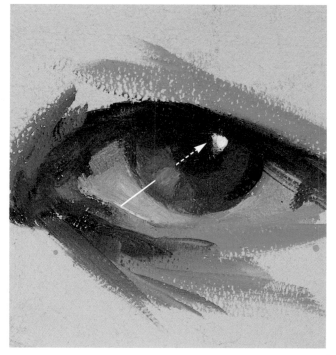

FIGURE 3.

Painting Glass

Colored glass has a mass tone, but it's entirely dependent on its background. The lighter the background, the lighter and brighter the bottle will appear; the darker the background, the darker the bottle will appear. No matter what background you use, however, the highlights won't change *(Figures 1 and 2).*

When beginning a painting of glass, disregard all the tones that you see on the front of the glass and record all the tones that you see on the rear side. By this I mean that these tones are caused by the background of the glass. If the glass is colorless, you actually use the colors that are in back of the glass, identified as *Figures 3* and *4. Figure 5* is the finished painting.

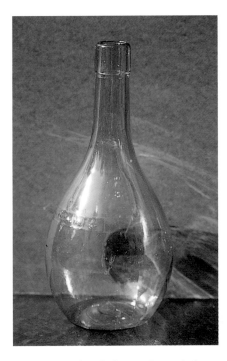

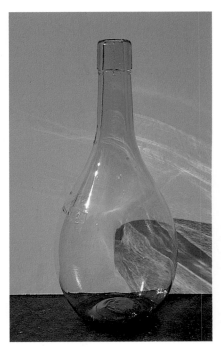

FIGURE 1. Colored Glass against a dark background.

FIGURE 2. Colored Glass against a light background.

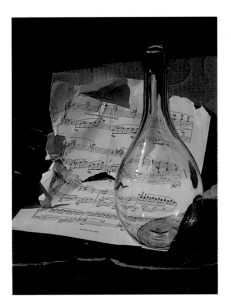

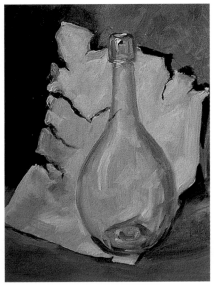

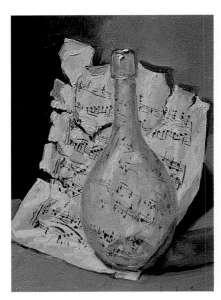

FIGURE 3.

FIGURE 4.

FIGURE 5.

Applying the Highlight

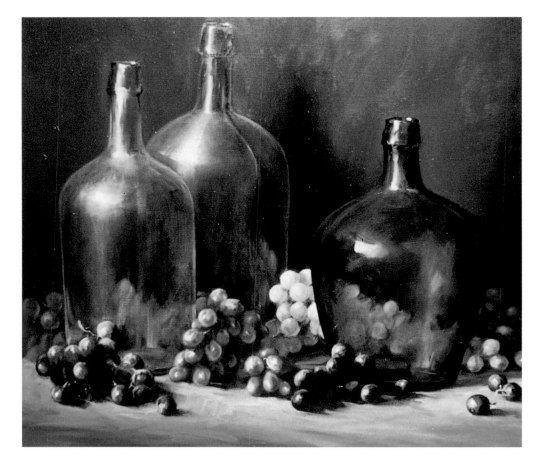

**Bottles and Fruit,
20 x 24",**
Private collection.
The highlights that appear here were all applied as I've just explained. All we see in this painting are the highlights as they have been fully refined.

The front view of glass is recorded by the highlight and reflections. It's important to remember that these reflections are gray and the highlight is white with a touch of the complement of the bottle's color. In the two illustrations shown here, the highlight is white with a touch of red, green's complement.

The gray reflection color is made by mixing black and white and a touch of the bottle color's complement. So, on a green bottle, the gray hazes — or reflections — are made with gray mixed with a little Indian Red, a complement of green.

To apply a highlight, first strike it on rather thickly *(Figure 1)*. Then, with a dry brush, fuzz it in *(Figure 2)*. Since this fuzzing usually mutes the highlight too much, the highlight will have to be applied again very carefully.

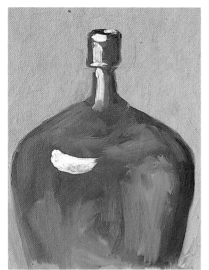

FIGURE 1.

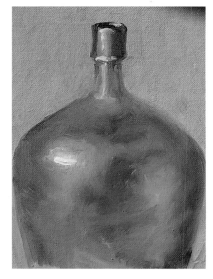

FIGURE 2.

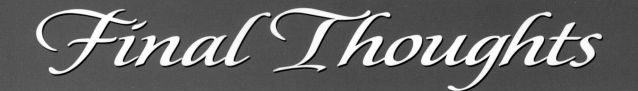

Final Thoughts

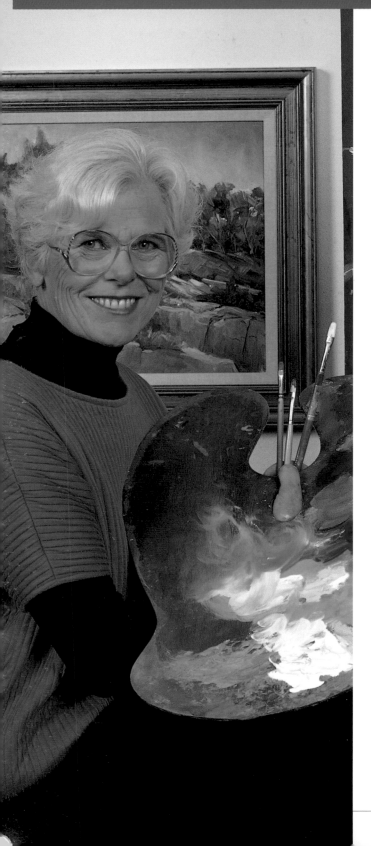

Helen Van Wyk's special gift for dispensing information and teaching principles to the painting populace has never been as much in evidence as in the pages you have just finished reading. She was proud of this book, when it first appeared in its black-and-white edition, and took great pleasure in the knowledge that readers referred to it as their bible. She would have been delighted with this up-dated, full-color revision of an enduring favorite.

These principles and procedures — the backbone of Helen's painting philosophy — are logical and valid. They have been embraced by a multitude of Helen's followers for more than forty years. If you were to apply them to your own paintings, we know that you would benefit from them. The wisdom of Helen's fundamental principles can only be effective if, along with the painting techniques it teaches, it will also make you solve for yourself the stew of problems that only a complicated craft like painting could stir up. Good Luck!

— *The Publisher*

Index

List of Paintings

PAINTINGS BY HELEN VAN WYK

Ketchopoulos Market, 16 x 20" **6**

Study in White, 20 x 24" **10**

Flash's Toys, 14 x 18" **15**

Waiting for Life, 20 x 24" **16**

A Dutch Still Life, 12 x 16" **17**

Dutch Table Cover, 20 x 24" **20**

Bas Relief *(detail)*, 16 x 16" **34**

A Copper World, 20 x 24" **35**

First Corn of Summer *(detail)*,
    24 x 30" **38**

Indian Corn *(detail)*, 20 x 24" **39**

A Vegetable Medley *(detail)*,
    22 x 28" **40**

Garlic, 12 x 24" **41**

Iceberg and Lemon, 20 x 24" **44**

Beets, 20 x 24" **45**

Pears and Plums *(detail)*, 20 x 24" **47**

Lemons, 12 x 20" **48**

Bowl of Blueberries, 16 x 20" **49**

Strawberries *(detail)*, 12 x 16" **50**

Summer Fruit *(detail)*, 14 x 24" **51**

Pretty Kitty *(detail)*, 12 x 16" **52**

My Collie Beauty, 20 x 24" **53**

Irish Setter, 20 x 24" **55**

Big Sam, 20 x 24" **63**

JoAnn Gleason, 20 x 24" **64**

Patty Raskin *(detail)*, 20 x 24" **65**

Rembrandt's Woman Bathing
    (a copy), 11 x 15" **66**

Sunday Morning Diversion,
    20 x 24" **70**

Coconuts, 10 x 16" **73**

Old Books, 6 x 8" **73**

Tureen, 16 x 20" **73**

Porcelain Geese, 9 x 12" **74**

Mexican-made Cabinet, 16 x 20" **74**

Moses Bronze, 12 x 16" **74**

Books and Bayberry 12 x 20" **75**

Book and Pomegranate, 20 x 24" **75**

Corn and Beets, 20 x 24" **75**

Scallions and Cheese, 20 x 24" **80**

Books, 20 x 24" **81**

Antique Mandolin, 14 x 20" **81**

Spools of Thread, 4 x 6" **81**

Wrought Iron Pots, 20 x 24" **82**

Rockport Child, 16 x 16" **84**

Fountain in the Pincio, 20 x 24" **84**

Study of Books, 20 x 24" **84**

A Good Read, 16 x 20" **90**

Michael as Otello *(detail)*, 20 x 24" **98**

Woolen Table Cover, 20 x 24" **102**

Satin Drape, 20 x 24" **102**

Oak Bucket, 22 x 28" **105**

Jug and Pears, 22 x 28" **105**

Pitcher and Bowl, 20 x 24" **106**

Sculptured Pitcher *(detail)*,
    20 x 24" **107**

Cutwork Cloth, 20 x 24" **112**

Beer Stein and Music, 20 x 24" **115**

The Love Letter, 22 x 28" **115**

Strawberry Baskets, 18 x 24" **116**

Bottle and Fruit, 20 x 24" **123**

PAINTINGS BY LAURA ELKINS STOVER

Rockport Cottage, 16 x 20" **32**

Portrait of a Tapestry *(details)*,
    15 x 30" **33**

Eggshells, 3 x 6" **36**

Red Onions, 11 x 15" **43**

Still Life with Pumpkins, 16 x 20" **46**

The Carriage Fair, 9 x 12" **57**

Victorian Lady *(shown actual size)* **68**

Still Life with Indian Blanket,
    16 x 20" **72**

Still Life with Bread, 9 x 12" **82**

Books and Zinnias, 18 x 24" **88**

Bass Rocks, Gloucester, 16 x 20" **117**

INSTRUCTIONAL ILLUSTRATIONS BY LAURA ELKINS STOVER

Grapefruit **12**

Tangerine **13**

Plum Tomatoes **14**

Radishes **18**

Blue Vase **19**

Green Pitcher **19**

Moonlight **29**

Sheltie **56**

Phlox **58**

Delphinium **59**

Hydrangea **60**

Peonies **61**

Flowers **62**

Composition Sketches **77**

Composition Sketches **78**

Composition Sketches **79**

Ceramic Jug **89**

Nude Sculpture **94**

Roses **95**

Pewter Tankard **97**

Step-by-Step of Eyes **99**

Vase **100**

Silver Coffee Pot **103**

Texture Sketches **107**

Brush Manipulation **109**

Wood Textures **110**

Wood Textures **111**

Cutwork Cloth Sketches **113**

Sheet Music **117**

Drapery Sketches **120**

Glass and Sheet Music Sketches **122**

Helen Van Wyk Videos & Brushes

Now that you have an instruction book by Helen Van Wyk, you may want to fortify this information with Helen's eloquent demonstrations on video tape. Once you have viewed the techniques shown in the videos, you will understand why Helen Van Wyk is considered by multitudes of artists to be America's most effective teacher of realistic painting.

Brush Techniques: Your Painting's Handwriting

Universally recognized as the most important tool in painting, the brush remains a mystery in the hand of a painting beginner as well as in more experienced hands. In this one-hour video, Helen demonstrates how versatile brushes can be when used properly, for each painting you do. *60 Minutes, $24.95*

Oil Painting Techniques & Procedures

A two-hour demonstration of a still life. It starts with a monochromatic underpainting and is followed by glazing applications to end with direct *alla prima* touches. Finally, the technique of glazing is fully explained and illustrated. In this still life, you will see Helen paint every kind of texture which will help you with all the subject matter you may encounter in your still lifes. *120 Minutes, $49.95*

Painting Children from Photographs

At last, you can paint the child in your life without fuss and stress. This one-hour video shows you how to go about it. Helen tells you what kind of photographs are best suited to use as models. And once you're set on one, she explains, in easy-to-understand instructions, how to transfer it to canvas through the grid method. *60 Minutes, $24.95*

A Portrait: Step-by-Step

In this one-hour video, Helen covers every facet of portrait painting. You will learn about mixing the right flesh color, getting the shadow to look just right, and that difficult "turning edge," the area between light and shadow. If portraits are your interest, you won't want to miss this sterling, informative video. *60 Minutes, $39.95*

Elegant Abundance

During the 16th and 17th centuries, Dutch still life painters were producing masterpieces that were emblematic of the so-called Age of Elegance. In this 90-minute video, Helen recaptures that era with her superb still life that bursts with subjects and textures: lemons, silver, lobsters, glass, flowers, and more. If still life is your painting passion, you must own this stunning vehicle of instruction. *90 Minutes, $24.95*

Painting Flowers *Alla Prima*

Alla prima is an Italian phrase that means "all at once." In this one-hour presentation, Helen demonstrates this direct application of paint to interpret a bouquet of daisies. Throughout this video, you will learn how Helen gets her paint moist and juicy, a look that has entranced viewers of her TV show and live demonstrations. *60 Minutes, $39.95*

Kissing & Warm Colors

Encouraging us to think carefully about how we draw, Helen shows how "kissing" can make us confused about our subject. Helen teaches the "hot" subject of orange with a full demonstration of a still life that includes orange fruits and a vase.

The color is red, the subject is passion... Helen introduces us to still life involving leather books, wine glasses, covering lessons such as how to add passion to your paintings and how to paint reflections and glass. *75 Minutes, $29.95*

Strike a Pose

Helen studies and captures realistic flesh colors from a doll as if it were a real person, showing how you can capture the notoriously hard realism of skin. Helen tells us to ensure models are in a pose that relate to their personalities — more dominant people should be painted from below — the shy, from above denoting deference. *60 Minutes, $24.95*

Symphony of Light

Helen tackles the difficult shape and contours of a violin with a full demonstration and takes us through every step of the painting. You'll see how adding light and shadow will vastly improve your work and learn that is all achieved in a series of easy to follow stages. *60 Minutes, $24.95*

Conquering Earth & Water

With each stroke of Helen's brush you will learn to capture the feel, the light and the splendor of a close observation, whether it is a landscape or a seascape. Helen begins by painting a view from her studio and then moves onto a seascape where you'll learn to paint water crashing against rocks and make waves come alive. *60 Minutes, $24.95*

The Wonderful Color White

Helen shows you, through a complete demonstration, how to paint the color white and how useful it is. Covering color mixing and offering guidance about light & shade, this strangely interesting subject holds quite a few surprises as Helen paints a still life. The final lesson in this video covers snow, in particular its color, as Helen paints a winter scene of an old red barn. *75 Minutes, $29.95*

HELEN VAN WYK'S BRUSH SELECTIONS
The Overture Selection

This five-brush selection has been designed to serve you well throughout the development of your painting *right from its start*. They are made of a durable synthetic that won't curl or stretch. The soft-textured *Overture* brushes perform very much as sable brushes do but at a considerable fraction of their cost. *$36.95*

The Finale Selection

The five brushes in this selection were made specifically for the finishing touches of any painting. They are those parts of the painting that you usually are faced with from two-thirds done to the end: ornamental designs, highlights and, finally your precious, distinctive signature. What better name than *Finale*? *$31.95*

ORDER FORM

Please send me the videos/brushes I have checked below:

- [ ] Brush Techniques: Your Painting's Handwriting **$24.95**
- [ ] Oil Painting Techniques and Procedures **$49.95**
- [ ] Painting Children from Photographs **$24.95**
- [ ] A Portrait: Step-by-Step **$39.95**
- [ ] Elegant Abundance **$24.95**
- [ ] Painting Flowers "Alla Prima" **$39.95**
- [ ] Kissing & Warm Colors **$29.95**
- [ ] Strike a Pose **$24.95**
- [ ] Symphony of Light **$24.95**
- [ ] Conquering Earth & Water **$24.95**
- [ ] The Wonderful Color White **$29.95**
- [ ] Overture Brushes **$36.95**   [ ] Finale Brushes **$31.95**

Name _____

Address _____

City _____ State _____

Zip _____ Phone _____

[ ] Payment Enclosed $ _____ (or) Charge my [ ] Visa [ ] MasterCard

Add $4.50 Shipping & Handling.
Florida Residents Add 6% State Sales Tax.

Acct.# _____ Exp. Date _____

Signature _____